One

Majid advises industry and government on policy, strategy, and design for services. He recently served as an advisor within the Ministry of Economic Affairs and Climate in The Netherlands. There he co-founded a special unit called XLAB, developing new approaches to complex problems, and methods for visualizing systems, services, and transitions. He cut his teeth in sales and product management, before teaching, consulting, and design. After working for Carnegie Mellon, Gartner, and PwC, he has been on a mission to clarify the concept of a service. That led to this book. His other voyage of discovery is about patterns in food across cuisines and cultures. Three of his best fans call him dad.

Table of content

0

Opening

0

We approach the future with the lessons we learned in the past, and hope for the best – what else can we do?

Foreword

Our organizations face problems that are more open, complex, dynamic and networked than ever before. Services are often seen as a way forward for dealing with this new fluid reality. Decades ago we realized we should not approach the design of services using the same thinking that goes into the design of manufactured goods. However, to date we haven't really understood these differences. The fact that services are still represented as an evolution from goods has robbed us of the opportunity to fully grasp the very different reality of these ephemeral 'things' we call services. As a result, decades later, services *still* fail to meet our expectations – and they keep failing in entirely new and surprising ways.

This will not do.

The rise of services is accompanied by a rhetoric of digitalization, user experiences, and human-centered design. Digitalization does not change the fundamentals of a service whereas design flaws can be structural. Apart from being the most obvious things about services, user experiences do not fully account for customer dissatisfaction or delight. And, it turns out, when it comes to services, human-centered design only covers half the story. No wonder some of the best efforts in industry and government end in frustration. There must be other forces at play, and only through understanding them can we explain the paradoxes, conflicts, and unintended consequences that frustrate our efforts.

We urgently need to step back and do a complete rethink.

Services are much more complex than they seem. A clearer understanding of their structures and behaviors will enable us to devise thoughtful systems to design and implement them. Only then will we realize their full potential.

This book takes an unfamiliar path toward a new level of understanding. Along this path we hop, skip and jump on principles from mathematics, biology, and computer science, and use the guidance that we need from systems thinking, Gestalt psychology, and behavioral economics. The author exposes the internal structures of services using different models and metaphors for different perspectives. And as one of those rare structured thinkers in this space, he manages to build a new synthesis at the end.

Leafing through this book, the models and perspectives might look a bit daunting – this cannot be helped, they have to faithfully reflect the true complexity of services. The familiar examples help bring together theory and practice into a coherent whole. This is not a book to skim through, but one to delve into with curiosity and imagination. Think with it, link the insights to your own practices and you will be richly rewarded.

Kees Dorst
Sydney, Australia
July 24, 2018

This book is for a deeper understanding of what services are, what they can be, and why they even exist. Such an understanding put us in a better position to explain why services fail despite our best efforts. By studying failure, we can better understand success, or why some services dependably produce the value they promise, from the perspectives of customers and service providers. Any service that disproportionately benefits one side at the expense of the other will eventually fail, whatever the ulterior motives; for profit's sake or for public good.

Any solution is only as good as the thinking that goes into its design, development, and implementation. As solutions services are particularly prone to failure because the thinking is necessarily required on two sides. This book is a modest proposal on how to advance our thinking as customers and service providers; and as designers, engineers, lawyers, accountants, and consultants, or anyone who advises, assists, or works for either side.

Deepening our understanding tends to broaden it as we look across numerous examples to see what makes a service a service. Then we begin to notice that every service, no matter what kind, that ever was or ever will be, has the same structure based on a fixed number of elements that constitute design. A structure that is simple, complete, and universal enough to be represented in code. To a reader of this book that may be surprising, given the diversity in the fast expanding universe of services (Services come in so many different »sizes and shapes« so how can they all have the same structure?). But we only need to look at the concept of DNA in biology to recognize the possibility for expressing design as code. This is a major departure from the traditional thinking. It opens up exciting new possibilities for design and innovation in services. It is also a timely departure.

Technologies are transforming our worlds creating new possibilities and causing the universe of services – a solution space for societies' problems – to expand in new directions. For example, artificial intelligence, robotics, cloud computing, and the Internet of Things (IoT) are changing the way we pay for, provide, and make use of services that have been around for more than a century. They are also creating new services. The pace of change is mind boggling. However, current methods for designing services are based on a process mindset that became popular in the early 90s, and the principles of consumer marketing: Swim-lane dia-

Preface

grams mapping customer journeys across a front stage, in an open-loop left-to-right sequence, with procedure calls to layers in a back stage. While such methods are easy to learn and use, they lack the structure necessary to deal with challenges and opportunities at higher levels of complexity and scale.

Bohemian writer Franz Kafka has said: »If a book we are reading does not arouse us with a blow to the head, then why read it?«. While there is no danger of such violence, it suffices to say this book introduces a new way of thinking that may cause some collateral damage to popular preconceptions about services. It does so for a pragmatic purpose: To empower individuals and organizations to pursue bigger and bolder ideas in the form of services; rejecting false choices and compromises to create solutions that don't create new problems. As you go through this book there will be moments when the once familiar concept of a service becomes unfamiliar; even strange. Absent are some of the words we normally use to describe services. Those that are there, such as outcome, experience, and affordance, have new meanings.

The novelty is not for its own sake. In his book *Designing Design*, Japanese designer Kenya Hara suggests: »To understand something is not to be able to define it or describe it. Instead, taking something that we think we already know and making it unknown thrills us afresh with its reality and deepens our understanding of it.«

In a way, I am taking you through my own voyage of rediscovery that started 15 years ago at Carnegie Mellon University. I had been given the privilege to develop and teach a new course that prepares students to make a difference in the »service economy«. At the time, I was also part of a research project studying the capability maturity of service organizations. Multi-billion dollar outsourcing contracts were the trend. Customers and service providers were both wary of the hidden costs and risks in service contracts causing failures, reducing benefits, and eroding margins. The lack of a structural model made it difficult to find flaws until it was too late. I asked myself: If I put a 'tissue sample' of any service under a microscope, what would I see? I saw a triangular prism and that became my teaching model.

Years later, in 2010, while preparing to give a talk at the HP Services Research Lab in Palo Alto, California, I realized the prism

should actually be a cube. It had always troubled me that one edge of the prism was overloaded with two different meanings. Two prisms with a common base make a cube! Thus, I stumbled upon the duality of performance and affordance – the two ways in which every service produces value. The cube was my »double helix« model for explaining the idea of services having a genetic code. To prove the idea, I developed a method for describing the design of a service in a code-like format. I called it design//code.

Albert Einstein said: »If at first the idea is not absurd, then there is no hope for it«. At first things seemed hopeless. Wasn't my idea absurd enough? Luckily, I met Maarten Hillenaar, CIO of the Dutch Ministry of Internal Affairs and Kingdom Relations, and Hank Marquis at Lowe's. They were imaginative enough to see the potential and bold enough to apply an unproven method within their space. Boeing, UnitedHealthcare and the US Defense Information Systems Agency soon followed. The new now had friends. Together these pioneers also gave me a diverse set of problems to solve, that helped improve the method.

But it was during my time at RVO.NL, an agency of the Netherlands Ministry of Economic Affairs and Climate, that design//code evolved into a method called 16x. It is where, with Dounia Ouchene and Stephan Jenniskens, I co-founded a special unit called XLAB. Its mission is to help find new approaches to problems too complex for the core process, and to develop experimental methods that in future become part of the standard repertoire; 16x being one of them. My colleagues at RVO.NL, not only encouraged me to make 16x more useful in combination with storytelling, they also began using it to teach others the fundamentals of *denken in diensten*, or thinking in services. Watching them empower others with new knowledge partly inspired me to write this book.

Inspiration also came at the end of a 2015 workshop I ran in The Hague for the Ministry of Defense. I had used 30 cm cardboard cubes to teach the testing of hypotheses and the telling of stories to prove a service concept (X as a service). To convince their colleagues, participants gave values to the eight corners and edges of the cube, and then use those values to create a cogent narrative (Something you learn to do in the second half of this book). Even though they received a reference guide for 16x and the cube, one of them suggested I should also write a book. What kind of book?

A book that covers the fundamentals from which one can develop keener senses for services, be able to make better arguments, and develop new ideas and concepts. A book that teaches the 'first principles' based on which anyone can develop their own methods and templates rather than relying on »what's out there.« A book that on one hand forces you to think but on the other hand gives you templates, because as Buckminster Fuller said, »If you want to teach people a new way of thinking, don't bother trying to teach them. Instead, give them a tool, the use of which will lead to new ways of thinking.«

This is that book.

Part One: The first two chapters, »1 People« and »2 Things«, cover what services really are and why they even exist. After expanding the common definition of »service« with the concept of affordance, we get into the ethnography of things. That services are for people is quite obvious and commonly understood. But to truly understand why services exists we must understand things that people care about. We have already departed from conventional thinking. The next chapter, »3 Patterns«, introduces the most basic template for framing the concept of a service using two phrases, or 2x. Next, we learn how any service concept can be built up from or broken down into a set of patterns. We now have what we need to develop our own language and format for describing services.

Part Two: Over the next two chapters, »4 Promises« and »5 Factors«, we start by looking at how a set of four promises define the sides and aspects of every service and provides us the structural basis for the 4x frame. Then we highlight the internal structure of each promise by asking four simple questions. That leads us to the 16 elements that constitute the design of every service and form the 16x frame. The next chapter, »6 Elements«, briefly outlines the practical value of 16x and provides a 'parts catalog'. This chapter is more of a reference guide than a discussion. Chapter »7 Frames«, then gives us the practice we need to make effective use of 16x. By this point in the book we have learned a few techniques and acquired a powerful new template. With this new knowledge we can already communicate the concept of a service with new levels of clarity and depth.

Part Three: While every chapter of the book has its own look and feel (like the neighborhoods of Pittsburgh), the last two chapters may feel like an abrupt shift from the geometric progression of 2x, 4x and 16x. While all along we have been viewing services as systems, these two chapters are a gift for systems thinkers, policymakers, and strategists. The chapter, »8 Tensions« address the issue of net value and the tension between the three qualities of design – outcome, experience, and price. This chapter talks numbers. We begin to grasp the complexities that make designing services a challenge. The final chapter, »9 Tactics«, takes the concept of net value and maps it to a graph on which we visualize the dynamics of cooperation, conflict, and compromise, between customers and service providers. In doing so, we flirt with the idea of design as the ultimate expression of strategy, before closing this book.

This is a first attempt to share this new knowledge through a book. Please receive it with all the flaws and imperfections in my style of communicating. To get the most out of the book, please use the three things you have within you: your curiosity, imagination, and critical reasoning. Adding your own notes and observations then makes the book more complete – a single copy of a special edition.

Majid Iqbal
Utrecht, The Netherlands
July 24, 2018

Part

Clarity in concept cleanses the devil in the details.

1

People

1

We are born with the propensity for services. It is like a genetic predisposition. There isn't a vaccine for it.

Homo serviens

In his book *Sapiens: A Brief History of Humankind*, historian Yuval Noah Harari discusses the shift our species made from hunting and gathering to agriculture (Harari, 2015). The shift is thought to have occurred over a period of time, starting around 10000 BC. It led to tremendous growths in the *sapiens* populations, the invention of tools, development of new practices, and the first settlements. It also created new kinds of problems. Humans now had crops to tend and belongings to care for. They became specialized in tasks, getting better at them over time – a trend that continues to this day. However, specialization meant they had to depend on each other for things, and deal with each other like never before. Their lifestyles and diets became more dependent on fewer plants and animals. Living in close quarters gave rise to diseases that previously did not exist. By the time they were seen as problems, the dependency on agriculture was too high. There was no going back.

As a species we are far into a similar shift towards services. *The way our societies have evolved, not a single day goes by without paying for or making use of services.* Benefiting from or being subject to them. Or being a factor in their production. Our lifestyles have changed. We are busier than ever before, doing so many things at once. So many people to interact with and places to be. Many of those we may never visit. Many of them we may never meet. We cannot do it all, by ourselves – we are superspecialized now. So we depend on others more in a single day, than perhaps our ancestors did over an entire lifespan. We are *Homo serviens*. Life is normal with services. Indeed, after any major catastrophe, disaster, or strife, normalcy is said to be restored when services resume operations. For example, the electricity is back on, traffic lights are functioning, and the trains are running. The forces that restore normalcy are also services.

Services satisfy our needs. They are the only means to assure access to goods such as passports, licenses, and permits; healthcare, education, and social welfare; and justice, protection, and property rights. Some services are so basic – so much a part of our lives – we take them for granted. We expect them to be available to all regardless of income or social status, and at affordable prices, if not free of charge. We don't even think about them until they fail. Services stitch our social fabrics. As citizens and taxpayers, we pay for entire bundles of services, such as 'defense', 'foreign affairs', and 'intelligence'. We benefit from them even though we don't get to »use« them in the normal sense. We argue about how much to spend on them.[1]

Societies need services for every additional member. Even before we are born, our parents receive obstetric care, our health is monitored, and pictures are taken in ultrasound. Upon arrival into safe hands, we demand documentation – e.g., hospital records, birth certificates, social security cards, and insurance – even as we transfer from obstetrics to pediatric care. That point onwards, now and then, and for the rest of our lives, we create demand for services that have to do with documents. For example, those issuing passports, renewing licenses, notarizing deeds, and filing tax returns. That way, as »natural persons«, we create demand for many other lines of services, from the time we are born, till after we die.

The same is true when »legal persons« are born, whether as businesses, foundations, political campaigns, communities, charities, or trusts. They are born with the propensity for services – as they go about registering with authorities, raising capital, and advertising their offerings. More services are needed further on. Some needs are predictable and periodic, such as for processing payroll, tax filings, and rentals. But every up and down, twist and turn, expansion and contraction, also creates the demand for services. Corporations need services even as they cease to exist following acquisitions, bankruptcies, and dissolutions.

Services are solutions to many of our problems. Our propensity for them exists for many reasons. It isn't fixed. It varies over time. It depends on our realities, the opportunities we see within them, and our attempts to make the most out of them — using the things we have, and the things we don't. Our propensity also depends on the societies we participate in, our level of participation, and the resulting obligations — due to legal requirements, norms, and culture. We pay for or make use of some services often because that is what others expect us to do in particular situations.

Solutions to our problems

The propensity for services exists when people are unable to do certain tasks, such as surgical procedures, repairing faulty electrical circuits or drafting legal contracts. Where they are not lacking in skills or experience they face constraints that force them to delegate. For example, parents pay for childcare when they can't be at two places at the same time, and companies outsource administrative work to focus on core activities. In many cases, rules and regulations deny the do-it-yourself option, as in the case of security clearances, financial audits, and psychiatric evaluations requiring the unbiased opinion of third-parties.

Cannot, will not, do everything

The propensity for services exists where people perceive opportunity costs. Choosing transportation over driving somewhere gives them the opportunity to relax or get some work done. The propensity increases with income levels. As people attach higher values to their time, they delegate more kinds of tasks more often, such as housekeeping, dog walking, and grocery shopping. At the same time there are people willing to perform tasks others find boring, time-consuming, or laborious. They don't mind the extra money. In some countries, many of them have seen their income levels fall. Apps, maps, and routing algorithms are making it easier to find people on short notice. Thus, we have seen a growth in the *gig economy.*[2]

Like bionic exoskeletons, services artificially extend our range. Our ancestors would be surprised to see how easily we do what was impossible for them. We make things appear and disappear — sending and receiving them through thin air with simple gestures. Waving a card in front of a device seems to pay for stuff. Within a day or two we can be anywhere on the planet. When we arrive

Making possible the impossible

there, strangers give us what we want – not because they trust us, but the services that give us passports, visas, and credit cards. When we go on a road trip, highways, fueling stations, and telecom networks allow us to go even further. We can be at different places at the same time, moving toward a destination and at the same time making our presence felt elsewhere in high resolution.

Always be closing

The more services extend our range, the more we overreach. The more photos and videos we share, the more bandwidth and storage it takes. Digital services close the gaps so we create even more content and expect to access it from everywhere. Businesses make plans knowing there will be shortfalls in resources. They still go ahead. Services close the gaps with leases, loans, and lines of credit, college graduates, and flexible terms on office space. Those services in turn depend on other services to close *their* gaps and reduce operational risks. We have reinsurance for insurance, high schools for colleges, and construction for commercial real estate. Infrastructure services are closing gaps further ahead.

Things we have and things we don't

We cannot own everything. Not everything we can own is worth owning. We have the propensity for services because of the things we own and because of the things we don't. For example, if we own buildings, vehicles, or equipment, we pay for services that insure, protect and repair them. If we don't own those things, we pay for services that lease, rent, or share them. For the money we have, we use services that make it available to us through cash withdrawals or debit card transactions. For the money we don't have, credit card transactions. Thus, some services make the things we have more useful and valuable. Other services make things available to us when and where we need them the most.

The propensity for services exists because people want to get the most out of things. For example, whether we own a vehicle, lease, or rent it, we still pay for services that provide fuel, passage (through a bridge or tunnel), and parking. As more things enter our lives, we are even more in the markets for services. With new kinds of things, we depend on new kinds of services. We have services that make digital goods useable across devices, platforms, and other services. But digital goods can be more vulnerable to damage, loss, and theft than their physical analogues or equivalents. Therefore, we have services that protect privacy, data, and online experiences. We also have services that verify, maintain, and protect our digital keys, cash, and ID.

Services let people enjoy specific outcomes without owning (i.e. being held responsible for) certain costs and risks (Iqbal & Nieves, 2007). For example, airlines, hotels, and car rentals, bet on enough people not owning private jets, or homes and vehicles in every city they travel to. The costs and risks of maintaining such ownership positions would be too high for most. Stretching our imagination, the ridership of a public transit system is a loosely formed collective, with each rider *not-owning* a tiny fraction of the system, the moment they buy a ticket. Seen this way, services are what Harari calls imagined realities – legal fictions according to which complete strangers cooperate, coordinate, and exchange promises about owning and not-owning. With enough people not-owning, a service becomes viable. Risk aversion across entire geographies or populations may generate enough demand for the service. Enterprises see enough opportunity, reward, and purpose in assuming all such risk. They develop policies, strategies, and designs that reduce it to tolerable levels. Customers and service providers encourage each other with owning and not-owning, getting better at it over time. While service providers focus on the *total cost of ownership*, customers focus on the *total cost of utilization*. The latter includes the costs of finding, purchasing, and using the service. If the experiences are good the costs are low.

Ownership versus utilization

There is more software than ever before. More of it is *software-as-a-service*. Infrastructures such as airports, power grids, and payment networks have always been as-a-service. With cloud computing, we have *ephemeral* infrastructures, letting you to run software without caring for any of the several underlying layers. With sub-second metering, you pay only for the time their code is running – per 100 milliseconds and per call – like the time we did with public switched telephone networks. Instead of owning and maintaining costly critical components, airlines can subscribe to them. They pay per flight hour to gain access to spares pools and support services that guarantee availability and on time performance.[3] More things are as-a-service (e.g., music, bikes, and »birds«) partly because digital technologies are reducing the transaction costs – the cost of quickly and conveniently

Everything as a service

locating things, unlocking them, tracking their use, and loading them with credits or content.

Too small to notice

Hundreds of services run in the background when we are shopping online. Hundreds orchestrate action as a video on-demand service loads a profile, displays choices, and plays a selection. While reading news about a publicly-traded firm, the stock price a paragraph mentions, changes right before our eyes, as you're reading the story! And if we hover the mouse pointer over it, a graphic pops up right then and there, to show the price movement. Billions of profiles receive updates to their timelines and feeds as events are unfolding. Each profile renders unique, with personalized ads, content, and notifications. These inner workings are called microservices. They may be »too small to notice« but millions of them form the microbiome our daily lives depend on. Some are always on while others are active in short bursts and then they're gone. Many interact with each other, passing data, performing tasks, and displaying results. We are unaware of their existence. All we see are intermediate steps and some final outcome. It is magic.

Too big to fail

Imagine the difficulties around the world if the VISA payment network – with over 65000 messages per second – were unable to process card transactions for a day. Every day, air traffic control centers around the world guide a few hundred thousand flights from take-off to landing. Electricity, water, and data are always flowing. Which is why the critical infrastructures they run on fall within the scope of national security. Nobody thought Facebook was too big to fail until it did – failing to protect the data of millions of users from misuse, and failing to control the spread of fake news. During the 2008 financial crisis, the US government bailed out financial institutions on the following premise: their failure would expose millions of people to unbearable losses, including those who don't even use their services. In 2016, the future of the UK's national health service was part of the bitter debate that ended in the geopolitical crisis a.k.a. Brexit.

Problems with our solutions

Services solve many of our problems. They themselves are problems to solve. Some of those problems are relatively easy to solve. Others are like drug-resistant bacteria – they adapt to our problem solving approaches and evolve into new kinds of prob-

MULTYPLYING
ALL THE TIME

MULTYPLYING
ALL THE TIME

MULTYPLYING
ALL THE TIME

lems, multiplying all the time. Therefore, it is useful to understand the problematic nature of services, so we can design them to be much less of a problem to start with.

The dependency problem

Customers depend on services to close gaps for them. Where there is dependency there is risk; the probability of providers having what customers want, when and where they need it. Or, having enough of it because others may want the same thing, at the same time, or want it elsewhere. For providers, there is risk in depending on customers. They depend on customers depending on *them* and not others. Customers promise demand and providers promise supply. Services fail when either side fails to keep their promise. The very concept of a service requires several instances of demand from either a single customer or from several others with the same »custom« or habit (The original meaning of the word »customer« is someone who repeatedly comes back with the same need, problem or gap). The habit becomes stronger when a service more effectively fills the gap.

Service providers simply need to be sure enough there will be enough instances. They needn't all occur at the same time, for that could create another problem. Some services, as in healthcare and government, close gaps for large groups or populations. It is difficult to negotiate agreements with each individual. A single entity becomes the buyer on behalf of all those who make use of the service, or benefit from it. However, it is difficult to determine the needs, customs, and habits of a large number of users. There will be compromises. Some will be more happy than others. The dependency problem is also why only the simplest of services are profitable at planetary scales (e.g., payments, online search, and advertising). The needs are narrowly defined and simple, and there will always be demand, from someone somewhere on the planet.

The payment problem

There are services we pay for but don't seem to use, and services we use but don't seem to pay for. As individuals, we decide whether to pay for or make use of some services. With other services, we may not have a choice. We have to pay for or make use of them for being part of a population – as citizens we have to pay taxes, vote in elections, and have a valid ID. Most of us carry some form of payment. For employment, we go through background checks, training, and certification. Organizations submit to financial audits, credit ratings, and safety inspections, to meet legal requirements or maintain current status. Who pays, how much, and when, influence the feelings and attitudes of users, ranging from hostility, delight, and indifference.

Services that register property, enforce contracts, and settle disputes, create environments within which we can do business with strangers. Law enforcement services create artificial environments within which we feel safe. Other services protect natural environments, so we have clean air, water, and wilderness. Because of services that maintain roads, waterways, and airspace, we have mobility and transportation. The problem is when we cannot reconcile costs with benefits because of time separation – moments when we feel we are paying but don't seem to be benefiting, are separate in time from moments when we feel we are benefiting but don't seem to be paying. This causal ambiguity between costs and benefits can be problematic. Especially in the public sector.

The payment problem exists in another form. More than ever, we use services that are free of charge because commercial interests are paying for them (e.g., advertising). One could argue users are in fact paying – not in cash but in kind – because they are *paying* attention. They may also be paying with their privacy and personal data. That is clearer now since the implementation of the European General Data Protection Regulation (GDPR). Websites now display notices informing users they need to pay one way or the other. Whether informed consent is feasible or not, the problem with FREE is you don't know if you are paying too much.[4]

More often than not, services give us less than what we pay for. But that is not as obvious, or easy to prove, as in the case of buying goods and pointing to leakage, spoilage or damage. The problem is, the conflation of outcomes and experiences – two different things, inseparable. To get the outcome you have to go through the experience. For example, finding an option, buying the ticket, boarding the train, getting seated, the ticket check, and getting off the train, is the experience. Arriving on time at the destination is the outcome. We get less than the face value in the case of a pleasant experience but a late arrival. As in the case of an on-time arrival after a painful experience. However,

The valuation problem

the service provider may not see it that way, as long as they have brought you from »point A to point B«. There may be an apology but not a pro-rated refund.

In some cases, the outcome happens to be an experience. Take for example, a theatrical performance. Finding a show, purchasing a ticket, being ushered, and seated, is the service experience. Feeling amused, thrilled, or surprised – the wonderful experience – is the outcome. The pain we feel or »experience« during a medical procedure, is different from that which we feel while scheduling the visit, filling in the forms, and waiting to be seen. We tolerate the clerical pain – even though it is unnecessary as opposed to the clinical pain – because we care too much about the outcome. In general, we are more tolerant of lousy service experiences when we feel we don't have much choice (e.g., when going through airport security, getting a permit, or appearing in court).

Cooperation and trust

Every service requires arrangements for demand to meet supply. For that, customers and service providers have to cooperate with each other and coordinate action. Each side has to make an effort to make it easy for the other side to do what needs to be done. That involves an exchange that is fundamental to the very concept of a service. In particular, to the service experience. Depending on the type of service, this cooperative exchange may last a few seconds, several minutes, or hours or days. It is important for the two sides to trust each other, before »meeting« or soon after having »just met.« Each side gives the other custody and control of valuable things. The value may be sensitive to delay or damage. That includes the physical wellbeing, feelings, and rights of real people.

Think of a patient cooperating during clinical procedure and trusting there won't be medical errors, or accidental disclosure of personal information. Think of a stranger staying on your property. You expect them to treat it well – as if it were their own – without knowing in what state they have left their own home. Well, you cannot. Hence, with housekeeping, hotels let their guests enjoy, relax, and not worry about it too much. After all, not having to make your bed or pick up the towels is part of the appeal. If a guest causes too much damage, the hotel has their credit card on file. However, some kinds of damage are hard to prove or de-

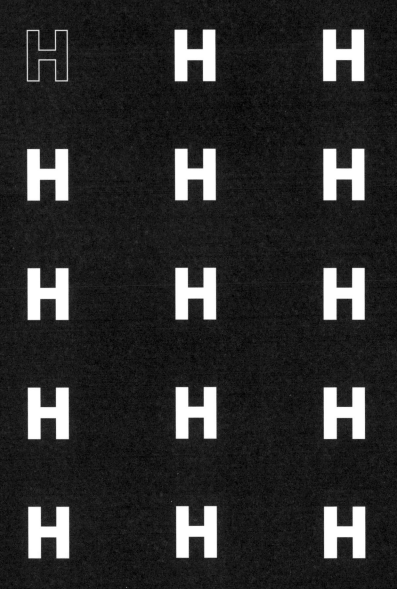

HUMAN ELEMENT

tect, or not until it is too late, especially when things are intangible. And controls may be too costly to implement.

The agency problem

Service providers employ agents to facilitate and control the use of the service. Agents help users get the most out of the service while enforcing agreements to protect the provider's interests. The design of every service requires agents – humans or machines – to be helpful, knowledgeable, and firm-handed. However, agents may fail in their duties due to their skills, stress, selfishness, and apathy or indifference. They may apply terms and conditions improperly, inconsistently or unfairly. When they are given discretionary authority to help customers in special circumstances, may abuse it to discriminate against people, due to prejudice. They may make things easier for themselves, or worse, enrich themselves. As a result, customers may get less than they paid for. Or, more than what was calculated in a cost model. In either case the provider has a problem.[5]

The agency problem also exists on the customer side. In many cases, those paying for a service are not the ones using it. User privileges are given to others, with the payer ultimately benefiting from the use. In such cases, users are effectively »customer agents«. Due to the agency problem we have overuse, misuse, and disuse. Overuse results in service charges that exceed budgets. It could happen, for example, to households with kids, enterprises with travel expenses, and health plans covered by insurance. Misuse is when the benefits of using the service do not accrue to the payer, even when within budget. Disuse is pure waste, due to users being indifferent.

Human nature

To reduce the agency problem in a service, customers and service providers favor more control. However, that may require more dialog and interaction between users and agents. As a result, the service may be costlier and less convenient. Controls often add steps to a sequence that adversely affect user experiences. The design of a control has to take into account the motivations and expectations on both sides. Behavioral sciences show how human nature can defeat the best of designs. Besides, the agency problem may persist at the contract level, between customers and providers.

Hospitals and physicians have been found guilty of overcharging for their services.[6] Banks have agreed to fines and settlements following lawsuits and regulatory action; for overdraft fees, discrimination in lending, and even fake accounts. Social media platforms, have agreed to do more to combat fake news, extremism, and the misuse of personal data. With advertising revenues, they have a conflict of interest. In one case, a private firm responsible for tracking people, was found to be fraudulently invoicing the government, for electronic tags on those who were either back in prison or already dead. Customers also misbehave. Universities deal with plagiarism, insurance companies with false claims, and banks with bad unpaid debts.

Automation

Automation plays an important role in the delivery of services. Self-service kiosks, vending machines, and payment terminals are given agency to act on behalf of the service provider. They need to be capable of dialog and interaction, and have the presence and influence necessary to facilitate and control the use of the service. However, despite advances in robotics, machine learning, and artificial intelligence, in many situations humans still have advantage. Therefore, service agents are most often combinations of both, with human-led or machine-led interfaces. The division of labor is important.

The design of a service distributes work between humans and machines, *and* between users and agents. That is a 'no-brainer' in some cases. Users and agents can both be machines. In other cases, just thinking about it can hurt the brain. Whether humans can be more effective in some situations, depends on several factors. Who the users are, the nature of the dialog and interaction, sensitivities, and subjectivities. Some societies and cultures may favor humans over machines. Rules and regulations may require users and agents to meet each other in person. Or, it may be the laws of physics.

What even is a service?

Ask six experts what a service is and they may give you six different explanations that are *not wrong* and then argue over the choice of words. Ask them what 'water' is and they may at least agree it is H2O. They may even explain why water behaves in the many different ways it does, because of the two hydrogen atoms forming a covalent bond with a single oxygen atom. Such scientific knowledge leads to solutions such as steam turbines, water picks, and hydrofoils. If water 'fails', we have a solid basis to find out why. There aren't any scientific definitions for 'service'. Legal definitions go back to the times when services were a form of 'consideration' that feudal tenants paid feudal lords. At one level, it may not matter. Everybody sort of knows what services are about. However, the answer to the question »What is even a service?«, can become important when, every now and then, we face the challenge of developing a new concept for a service, developing or improving a design, or figuring out why a service keeps failing. Then we sort of don't know.

However, instead of seeking a standard definition that is neither pedantic nor platonic, it may be good enough to just reach a temporary understanding about what services are, what they can be, and why they even exist. We are then free to maintain this understanding or discard it. We can be as imaginative as we want, not worrying about running afoul of established theories and frameworks. To help us form one such understanding for the duration of this book, we enlist the help of two professional skeptics: Thomas Doubting and Jerry Maguire. Give them any idea or concept and they will criticize it. They make arguments that lead to a better understanding. So, here's how it works. We start by making a simple statement about services. They criticize it. We modify the statement. They challenge us again. Through the ensuing back-and-forth we arrive at a new understanding which we then carry further.

»Services satisfy a set of needs.«

»Services satisfy a set of needs.«

Tom   Oh, come on. Give us something.

»Services are performances that satisfy a set of needs.«

»Services are performances that satisfy a set of needs.«

Tom   Ok, they perform an activity that satisfies a set of needs.[7]
Jerry   But it's not just performances is it? Services also make things available to us. For example, the goods on shelves of a grocery store, office space for rent, or a seat on the tram that will take me somewhere. Availability matters more than any activity itself.
Tom   Wait, moving people is clearly a performance.
Jerry   I don't care how moving the performance may be, if there isn't a seat for me, or if it is going to be too long

of a wait before the next ride, or if my destination is not even on the route. As Lucius Burckhardt said, »It is not the tram that makes transportation a successful experience. It is the schedule.«

Tom   Lucius who?

Jerry   He was a Swiss sociologist and economist. You should read more.

Tom   I agree. Not about the reading more often, but about services being more than just performances. When I borrow money, it's the loan amount and period that matter, not the lending process.

»Services are performances and affordances that satisfy a set of needs.«

»Services are performances and affordances that satisfy a set of needs.«

Jerry   That's interesting. I like the idea of using 'affordance' to describe services, especially if it is the Gibson ...[8]

Tom   Affordability?

Jerry   No, not affordability. A-F-F-O-R-D-A-N-C-E. To *afford* means to offer, to provide, to make available, to allow, to furnish or supply ...

Tom   You mean ...

Author   Let him finish.

Jerry   Thank you. Yes, Tom, please afford me the opportunity of finishing my sentences. Provide me silence. Allow me to explain that to afford also means to accommodate someone or something within an environment. For example, when you rent a safe deposit box or locker at a bank, you are given access to a container for you to store your valuables in. From being situated within the bank's vault, the space inside the locker is part of a secure environment. The bank goes to the necessary lengths to protect the vault. Therefore, anything the accountholder places inside the locker is *afforded* a certain level of security. The larger the locker, the greater the affordance. Every layer of protection the bank applies to the vault, including fire protection, adds to the affordance in proportion to the space inside. Since it is not possible to open the locker without the accountholder's private key, privacy is also a part of the affordance.

Tom   But transportation.

Jerry   When you purchase a ticket for the tram, it first gives you access to the entire schedule. It allows you to board any

Figure 1
Nested affordances

A Locker
B Vault
C Building
D Neighborhood

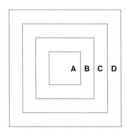

tram you want, or the next available one. Then, the ticket allows you to occupy any available seat or standing space, except the driver's seat of course. There are seats reserved for the disabled, the elderly, and the pregnant. Those are affordances themselves, as are the areas marked for bikes, strollers, and luggage. Affordances within affordances bundled together and paid for by a single ticket.

Tom   That is why airlines are able to unbundle offerings, charging you separately for seats and checked baggage.

Jerry   Yes, in a way. Affordances can also be sold in terms of which seat a passenger can occupy, in which cabin, or class of fare. There are restrictions on how much you can bring on board in terms of weight and dimensions, and what you are not allowed to carry as per the regulations. Therefore, inherent in the concept of affordance are degrees, limits, and restrictions, because of the costs and risks incurred by the environment.

Tom   So, when a bank lends me money, their balance sheet accommodates the risk and carries my debt.

Jerry   That's a good leap. The same is true of risk pools in insurance. It is what services do: Assume certain costs and risks inherent in demand. Hotels have policies that deter guests from smoking in rooms during their stay. Car rental companies require some form of collateral. It is a fair deal. Once their needs are met, customers get to walk away from it all without further obligations.

»Services are performances and ...«

Tom   I get it. Affordances are the basis of pricing service options. For example, how many gigabytes of data I'm allowed per month, or how many miles a year on a leased vehicle. I also get how when I can't afford to pay for something, it means my budget »doesn't allow for it«.

Jerry   He is a quick learner ...

Tom   I have the capacity for abstract thought.

Jerry   O' Brother ...

Tom   Okay ... moving on.

»Services are performances
and affordances that satisfy
a set of needs.«

»Services are performances and affordances that satisfy a set of needs.«

Jerry   Pithy!

Tom   Pity it doesn't clarify something very important. Allow
       me to explain. I have a washing machine at home I throw
       dirty laundry into. Then, upon my command, this appli-
       ance washes my clothes for me without complaint. The
       washing, rinsing and spinning form the performance.
       The capacity of the drum and the various wash cycles
       form the affordance, including the convenience of the
       machine being situated at home. I have access to it any
       time I want. The machine fulfills a set of needs: clean-
       ing my clothes quickly and thoroughly enough without
       causing damage to the fabric. But that doesn't make it a
       service for two reasons in my opinion.
Jerry And those are?
Tom   First, I bear all the costs and risks of owning and oper-
       ating the machine. I supply the electricity, water and de-
       tergent. If the machine breaks down for some reason, I
       have to take care of the maintenance. When the machine
       is idle, it takes up valuable space. Second, even though
       I don't pay the machine for the work, it doesn't have a
       choice but to serve me. That is servitude, not a service.
       In contrast, a coin-operated laundry machine provides a
       service because I pay for the wash cycles I use, and the
       machine can refuse to operate without payment. The
       hardware of the coin mechanism implements the primi-
       tive ancestor of a smart contract (Szabo, 1996).
Jerry So, in theory, if a company were to own the machine in
       your house (with a mechanism that tracks usage) and
       charge you for it, you'd consider it a service.
Tom   Yes. In that scenario they would also supply detergent,
       perform maintenance, and replace the machine, say ev-
       ery two years, for me to take advantage of technological
       advances. The service may not be economically viable for
       them, unless perhaps it also includes subscriptions to the
       oven and fridge. The appliances themselves aren't that
       expensive to own and operate compared to an automobile.[9]
Jerry Getting back to the statement, what simple change are
       you proposing?
Tom   I suggest we include a reference that implies there is
       some form of payment or consideration in cash or in
       kind. That way the statement is true of services offered
       free of charge such as Google, Facebook and Twitter al-
       though I don't think their »users« are in fact customers.

»Services are performances
and affordances that satisfy a
set of customer needs.«

»Services are performances and affordances that satisfy a set of customer needs.«

Tom   That will do.

Jerry   Hmm. What about experiences? They are a defining
        characteristic of services.

Tom   Perhaps you are right, but I think it is more important to
        emphasize outcomes. What am I buying when I pay for
        that tram ticket? Being somewhere within a certain time-
        frame. The experience of riding the tram is what I have to
        go through to get there. I would like that to be a good ex-
        perience but more than that I'd appreciate the outcome.
        Every centimeter the tram moves toward the destination,
        I get a bit more of what I paid for. I wouldn't travel further
        than my destination just because it is a good experience.

Jerry   But the experience matters a lot. Say the next tram
        is about to arrive, and within 30 seconds I am able to
        quickly purchase a ticket at the tram stop, because
        they make it effortless. There are ticket machines,
        which accept several forms of payments. A smart-
        phone app makes it very easy to know if that's the tram
        I should be stepping into. No more missing the tram
        from still trying to figure that out, by asking around, or
        by trying to read from a printed schedule or map. I agree
        the outcome I am paying for is being somewhere, but
        the journey needs to be safe and comfortable as well.
        The spaciousness of the tram car, the seats, the grips,
        the windows, the lighting, and even the shocks. Other-
        wise, I wouldn't want to ride the tram at all. I'd call a cab
        or something.

Tom   In this example, the »things« being transported are
        people with feelings – sensitive things. Their subjective
        evaluation of the travel experience can get mixed with
        that of the outcome. Whereas when we ship a package,
        we limit our evaluation of the experience to the send-
        ing, receiving, tracking, and paying for the shipment. We
        don't ask the thing we shipped inside the package how
        good its travel experience was.

Jerry   *Outcomes are what you pay for and experience is
        what you pay with.* If the experience is better than ex-
        pected, then it feels like a discount or rebate.

Tom   Yes. I don't get what I paid for if the tram doesn't take
        me there within a certain timeframe. The tram arrives

on time, not just for the people waiting to step in, but more importantly, for those stepping out. I think that's why your friend Lucius emphasizes the schedule in that quote, although he should have used the word »outcome« instead of »experience«. More than linking places across the city, what the schedule does is link time slots, offering thousands of combinations that coincide with journeys people want to make.[10]

Jerry   So, where are we then?

»Services are performances and affordances resulting in outcomes that satisfy a set of cutomer needs.«

»Services are performances and affordances resulting in outcomes that satisfy a set of customer needs.«

Jerry   As long as it doesn't seem like we are downplaying the importance of the quality of experience.

Tom   But we are not, and I believe people are smart enough to know what is implied or left out.[11]

Jerry   Fair enough. I suggest we use the word 'producing' instead of 'resulting' because the outcomes are the products of performance and affordance. I know people are accustomed to saying 'products and services'. But services *are* products. We have product managers, product roadmaps, and product backlogs. The gross domestic product (GDP) number covers both goods *and* services.

Tom   The word also hints at the production behind the service, the designs, planning, and other practical considerations without which the performances and affordances are just theoretical possibilities. But why a *set* of needs? Why not just 'needs'?

Jerry   Because, your need »to be« somewhere comes with the need »to have« a seat on the tram. Your valuables need »to be« protected and therefore you need »to have« a space inside the vault. To fulfill a physician's need to have insight into a patient's health condition, the patient's anatomical detail needs to be scanned. The two types of needs go hand in hand. Therefore a *set* of needs.

Tom   Ok, got it.

»Services are performances and affordances producing outcomes that satisfy a set of customer needs.«

»Services are performances and affordances producing outcomes that satisfy a set of customer needs.«

Jerry   Good enough.
Tom   For now.

OUTCOMES ARE WHAT YOU PAY FOR

EXPERIENCE
IS WHAT YOU
PAY WITH

2

Things

2

Things store the potential for services.

What sort of things? All sorts of things. Tangible and intangible things. Things that move across time and space. Those that stay put or stand in place. Things we place on a shelf or a table. Things that act like a pipe or cable. From trains, tracks, and transmission lines, to privacy, privilege, and peace of mind. Things we share, in files and formats, and those we leave under dusty doormats. Things big and small, expensive and cheap. Things for daily use that we hardly ever keep. Things that, when you drop them, they make a sound. Things that won't turn up at the lost and found. Things that unlock with a finger's touch. Things that when taken away, it hurts very much. Things that when they're valid they signal status, to the controlling logic of some apparatus. Things that vibrate when someone calls. There is service potential in them all.

You have created a beautiful illustration. It is a work of art. A digital asset that by itself is useful and valuable on websites or as part of a keynote presentation. It isn't until you want to display copies of it on walls that the shortcoming and shortfall emerge. The illustration needs to be printed in the size and format of large posters, and it needs to have the right quality and amount of ink and paper. You may have the capabilities and resources for making posters. It is also likely you procure the services of a printer. Otherwise, the digital file by itself has neither deficiency nor defect. The same is true for example, of an aircraft, recipe, vote, property, bank balance, passport, speech and a knee. They are tangible and intangible assets that, when placed in a context of use or situation, might feel uncertain, unrecognized, under-appreciated, unprotected, underutilized, or unable to function. Thus, they store the potential for services.

Figure 2
Things

Some things store the potential for performances.

Thing → needs to be → therefore
Bank balance → in the form of currency notes → cash with drawal
Passport → stamped → border checkpoint
Speech → translated → live translation
Knee → examined → medical imaging

Thing → is able to → therefore
ATM → convert an amount into currency notes → cash with drawal
Authority vested → validate documents → border checkpoint
Multilingual mind → translate speeches → live translation
MRI scanner → capture a health condition → medical imaging

Some things store the potential for affordances.

Thing → needs to have → therefore
Aircraft → 3000 meter long strip of asphalt → safe landing
Recipe → ingredients → grocery purchase
Vote → a ballot → election
Property → financial coverage → insurance policy

Thing → is able to → therefore
Runway → cover a run up to 3800 m long → safe landing
Store shelf → carry an assortment of goods → grocery purchase
Ballot → record vote on official paper → election
Risk pool → absorb losses from damage → insurance policy

Ok, so things store the potential for services. But that potential won't become actual until and unless those things are part of an arrangement, or simply put, come in »contact« with each other. Here, by »arrangement« we mean the things put together, placed in position, or configured in a way that allows for something specific to happen as part of a plan or agreement. The arrangements do not just happen.

Arrangements

The ATM machine needs to verify the bank balance, to convert a portion of it into the currency notes it then dispenses from its safe. Somehow the officer's authority and judgment have to come into contact with the visa privilege – two intangible things in physical contact, as is clear from the sound of the passport being stamped. The multilingual mind of a translator has to listen to the speaker at the podium and absorb what is being said a fraction of a second quicker than everybody else, to immediately give voice to her live translation.[12] The patient's knee has to be inside the MRI scanner; wrapped with special antenna coils and carefully positioned to capture radio signals from the tissue being examined. The aircraft gracefully descends upon the runway which is kept clear of all other traffic. Grocery stores fill their shelves with things people are mostly likely to run out of when planning to cook a meal. Lifestyles, diets and recipes go into models that determine how to best stock those shelves with an assortment of goods. Ballots are the »official paper« that record citizens' votes to make them count. Through an insurance policy, a house, boat, or tool shed is linked to a mathematically modeled pool of risk.

Aircraft – Runway
Recipe – Shelf
Vote – Ballot
Property – Risk Pool
Bank balance – ATM
Passport – Authority
Speech – Multilingual mind
Knee – MRI Scanner

Customers care about services because of things they consider to be useful and valuable – assets that produce a stream of benefits.[13] However, there are situations in which those things aren't able to realize their full potential. In those situations, they become needy things, or things with shortcomings and shortfalls. Approaching aircraft can fly in circles, but airlines and pilots would prefer they soon have an assigned runway and cleared to land. The bank can safely hold the money for future use, but the accountholder may prefer that some of the money is immediately available for spending. Uninsured property is still property, but the owners would prefer that it is insured against future loss or expense. One can make similar arguments about why other things such as the vote, recipe, speech, passport and the knee create the need for services.

Services make people better off, or *not worse off*. If we were to appropriate Herbert Simon's definition of what it means »to design«, and apply it to services, we could say, »services are devised courses of action aimed at changing existing situations into preferred ones, in which things are more useful and valuable« (Simon, 1996). In other words, services not natural phenomenon. Services are *by design*. Services *are* designs.

Four types of things

There are two types of arrangements. We can label them X and Y : X for affordance and Y for performance. There are two sides to each arrangement. We can label them - and + , like the terminals of a battery: - for demand and + for supply. Opposites attract.

-	Aircraft	X	Runway	+
-	Recipe	X	Shelf	+
-	Vote	X	Ballot	+
-	Property	X	Risk Pool	+
-	Bank balance	Y	ATM	+
-	Passport	Y	Authority	+
-	Speech	Y	Multilingual Mind	+
-	Knee	Y	MRI Scanner	+

Therefore, we have *four types of things* in every service:

Artifacts [e.g., Bank balance, passport, speech, knee, ...] Y-
Events [e.g., Aircraft, recipe, property, vote, ...] X-
Capabilities [e.g., ATM, authority, mind, MRI scanner, ...] Y+
Resources [e.g., Runway, store shelf, ballot, risk pool, ...] X+

Artifacts and events are what customers bring to the demand side of the arrangements. Capabilities and resources are things service providers put in place, on the supply-side of arrangements, keeping in mind the needs of artifacts and events.

Artifacts are things with shortcomings. They express their needs in the form of tasks to be performed.

- Artifact → task
- Bank balance → convert to currency notes
- Passport → place a stamp that validates privileges
- Speech → translate to another language
- Knee → capture a high-resolution image

Events are things with shortfalls. They express their needs in terms of having access to resources.[14]

- Event → access to
- Aircraft → a long enough runway on which to land
- Recipe → ingredients in the right amount
- Vote → a ballot on which to record vote
- Property → financial reserves that cover losses

Capabilities are things with skills. They *fix* shortcomings through activities that perform tasks.

+ Capability → activity
+ ATM → dispensing currency notes in necessary amounts
+ Authority vested → granting entry privileges
+ Multilingual mind → translating a live speech
+ MRI scanner → scanning specified areas

Resources are things with surpluses. They *fill* the shortfalls through availabilities. For access.

+ Resource → availability
+ Runway → allowing large wide-body aircraft to land
+ Store shelf → displaying an assortment of goods for sale
+ Ballot → allowing the official recording of a vote
+ Risk pool → covering losses from damage

While capabilities, resources, artifacts, and events – the four types of things – store the potential for a service, it is *availability, activity, access and task* that are the actual instances of demand and supply. Artifacts and events broadcast their needs to the world around them, telling other things they have jobs to be done. They advertise their tasks and (the need for) access, thinking out loud for any capabilities and resources out there that may be listening. Similarly, capabilities and resources broadcast their abilities, advertising their activities and availabilities, for any artifacts and events listening.

Figure 3
Job advertisements

Affordance (X) ——
Performance (Y) ——

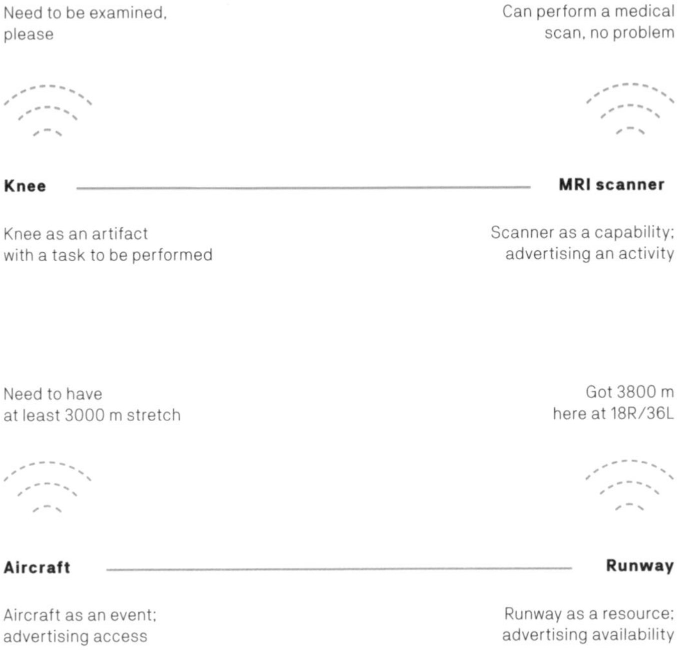

Need to be examined, please

Can perform a medical scan, no problem

Knee ————————————————————— **MRI scanner**

Knee as an artifact with a task to be performed

Scanner as a capability; advertising an activity

Need to have at least 3000 m stretch

Got 3800 m here at 18R/36L

Aircraft ————————————————————— **Runway**

Aircraft as an event; advertising access

Runway as a resource; advertising availability

This and that

»You think because you understand ‚one' you also understand ‚two', because one and one make two. But you must also understand ‚and'.«

—

Maulana Jalal ad-Din Muhammad Rumi, 13th century poet, jurist and scholar

Access and task together define the demand for the service. Availability and activity define supply. Availability and access together define affordances.[15] Activity and task together define performances.

X-, Y-	Access	and	task	define	demand
X+, Y+	Availability	and	activity	define	supply
X+, X-	Availability	and	access	define	affordance
Y+, Y-	Activity	and	task	define	performance

Artifacts and events depend on capabilities and resources to render them to preferred conditions and states. Things aren't capabilities and resources if they cannot dependably produce that desired effect. In some cases, the dependencies are so strong they are visible in the designs of artifacts and events. In the design of an electric vehicle, for example, we see the charging station that supplies energy, diagnostic instruments that plug in to gather data, and the hook of a towing truck. Mobile phones are embedded with chips that allow them to connect to cellular networks. The charger, instrument, hook, and signal are *absent assets* – things taken for granted and accounted for in the design of artifacts and events.

The reverse is also true. Take ground services at airports for example. Everything, from policies, procedures, and protocols, to equipment, facilities, and infrastructure are designed around the aircraft they support. It is aircraft-centered design.[16] In other words, aircraft are the artifacts and events, around which services in that ecosystem are designed. Software applications have API, or application programming interfaces, through which they accept requests and provide responses. Things in the outside world that depend on those applications to make something available, or get something done, interact with them through the API. We can generalize the concept to say that the four types of things in a service interact with each other through »affordance performance interfaces«.

In services, instances of demand and supply create windows of opportunity for each other, across space and time. The timing and duration of a window of opportunity vary based on the type of performances and affordances. The windows may open and close according to a schedule. They may frequently occur, or once in a while. The durations could be for years, months, and days or hours, minutes, and seconds. High-frequency trading systems on Wall Street execute multiple trades within a fraction of a second. Compare that to a phone call that lasts a few minutes, the hourly parking, the next-day delivery of a package, or the monthly subscription to a newspaper, and a multi-year lease of a building or facility.

Windows of opportunity

»Thirty spokes share the wheel's hub; It is the center hole that makes it useful. Shape clay into a vessel; It is the space within that makes it useful. Only because of what is not there, it is possible that there is what is there; and only because of what is there it is possible that there is not what is not there.«

—

Lao Tsu

Instances of supply appear *within* instances of demand, or vice versa. Think of the Netflix subscriber deciding to watch a movie at home or wherever. The video immediately starts playing at the touch of a button. Software within Netflix's global infrastructure creates a movie instance, streaming it from a copy of a master file, at a bit rate dynamically optimized for the subscriber's device, screen size, and Internet speed. Compare that with cinema-goers settling down in their seats just in time with drinks and popcorn; instances of demand appearing within an instance of supply. To more effectively fulfill a set of a needs, service providers must anticipate customer needs, plan investments, and put things in place ahead of time. It is part of *strategic design*. How far ahead depends on the nature of the underlying capacities. Regardless of the planning horizon, service providers have to truly understand why certain shortcomings and shortfalls exist at a particular time and place, the windows of opportunity, and the opening and closing patterns.

Figure 4
Windows of opportunity

Ethnography of things

The principles of human-centered design require us to have deep empathy with the people we are designing services for, by immersing ourselves in their lives. We study the social interactions, behaviors, and perceptions within groups, communities, and organizations. As ethnographers, we spend a lot of time with the stakeholders of a service, including users and agents; long enough to understand and document social arrangements and belief systems. Detailed observations and interviews allow us to gain insights into their views and actions within situations, surroundings, and environments (Reeves, Kuper, & Hodges, 2008).

Elisa Giaccardi and Iohanna Nicenboim, at the Delft University of Technology (TU/Delft), Chris Speed, at the University of Edinburgh, and Nazli Cila, at the Hogeschool van Amsterdam, are among a group of researchers who study things like they study people. Through the *ethnography of things*, they study social arrangements between things such as the kettle, fridge, and cup within the context of a daily routine such as »making coffee«. They interview things. They study the dispositions, dependencies, and interactions, recording their observations on *object persona* templates.

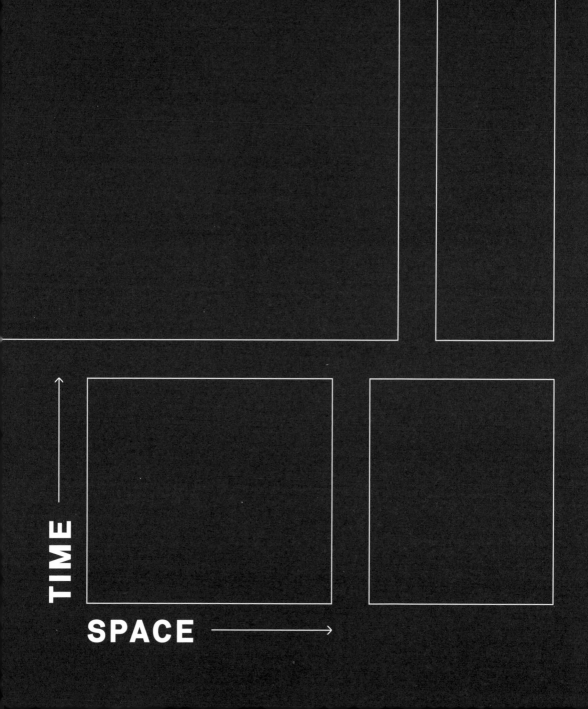

»*Objects are our witnesses, companions, and accomplices in our everyday life practices. They manifest how we experience the world around us, how we think, and which values we hold dear ... by generating object personas, designers can look into an object's life and out to the social contexts in which the object exists to obtain a better understanding of the object and its use practices.*«

—

Cila, Giaccardi, Tynan-O'Mahony, & Speed, 2015

Thing-Centered Design started as a way of exploring the creative possibilities of the Internet of Things. As objects around us begin to collect data and make suggestions about what might be desirable, they may point to possibilities we may otherwise never think of (Giaccardi, Cila, Speed, & Caldwell, 2016b). The researchers fit things with cameras and sensors to acquire data.[17] Visualization of the data reveals the movements and placements of those objects across space and time – behavioral patterns, temporal routines, and spatial movements of objects and their users – leading to new insight.

Many such objects are part of services, as one or more of the four types of things. Things with shortcomings and shortfalls attract things with skills and surpluses. Capabilities attract artifacts. Resources attract events. The four types of things form social arrangements, as part of a »belief system« – a set of four promises that, as we shall see, are the basis of service agreements. By studying the social life of useful and valuable things, we can design services better. By personifying things, and studying them the way we study people, we discover new potential for performances and affordances, and more clearly see limits and constraints; recognizing why some arrangements are possible but actually not permitted.

Figure 5
Objects as witnesses

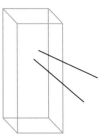

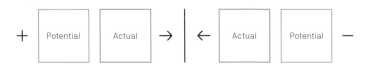

Dangerous liaisons

For example, hazardous materials can be loaded into the hold of an aircraft but not permitted. Electronic health records can be stored and displayed on many kinds of devices but are limited to those that comply with rules and regulations governing protected health information. More things are digital. More data is being gathered than ever before across mobile devices and platforms. More of it is at risk. Hackers steal data on millions of customers from a single breach. Recent revelations about the extent to which social networks have allowed third-parties gain access to personal data and misuse it, further underscore the importance of seeing services from the perspective of things. Informed consent or not, for the affordances in question, the user data is on the supply side of an arrangement; not as an event as one might think, but as a resource for paying customers.

Service industries are often early adopters of new technologies with the aim of offering superior outcomes and experiences. That tradition continues with advances in artificial intelligence, robotics, and the Internet of Things. Things are assuming new roles and responsibilities. On roads, »driver things« made of software, sensors, and machine learning, are being designed to take control of the driving from tired, distracted, and impatient humans. The future may be promising, but the early versions have been prone to error, underscoring the ethical dilemmas and unaddressed legal issues such as insurance and liability – important matters for manufacturers, customers and service providers. Inside homes, devices such as Alexa, Siri and Google Home are things pretending to be people – attentive, helpful, and obedient members of a household, with »good connections« and happy to be entrusted with more chores. They are living amongst people, interviewing them, listening to everything, and gathering data – developing rich and holistic insights, not just to make things easy for the household but also to be exploited by third-parties for commercial purposes. They are ethnographers! We need to study them better before we allow them to study us further.

As we find ourselves solving problems and imagining new futures, our increasingly complex environments of needs, requirements, and constraints, require us to have interdisciplinary teams with a transdisciplinary focus (Dorst, 2015). *Services are arrangements and agreements – agreements between people about the arrangements between things.* Therefore, designing services requires us to at once focus on humans and things, using the skills, practices, and tools of human-centered design and thing-centered design.

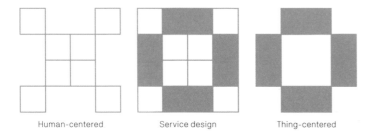

Human-centered   Service design   Thing-centered

Figure 6
Human-centered *and*
Thing-centered

Alice in Nederland

Alice is on the inter-city train from Utrecht to the Amsterdam Schiphol airport, seated in a first-class compartment. She is listening to music, sipping a coffee, and reading news. The music is from the Daily Mix made for her by Spotify. It includes her favorites and suggestions from a recommendation algorithm. *It is an endless mix. More songs load as she listens.* As the train crosses the Amsterdam-Rhine canal, she gets notifications on her smartphone. Before she has time to take a look, she is politely interrupted by the ticket conductor. She hands over her OV chipkaart, which is an electronic travel pass loaded with the ticket for the journey. It can be used across all modes of public transport in the Netherlands, including bicycles for rent. The conductor holds the card to a hand-held terminal, to see whether Alice has checked in at the station before boarding the train, as all passengers are required to do, and if she has loaded the first-class option. Alice is using the type of card that employers provide for work-related travel, allowing for the charges to be paid by a corporate account. Time to take a look at those notifications.

She has received a few »likes« on the tweet she had posted a few minutes earlier. One of the notifications is from Dropbox, a digital service that facilitates collaboration among people through the sharing of files. Every time a user creates, modifies, or deletes a file in a shared folder, the service instantly updates everyone's copies and sends them notifications. Most crucially, it provides the necessary storage in a way that allows users to access those files from any connected device. Alice opens one of the files, typing in a few changes, and adds a comment. As she closes the document, the Dropbox agent (a piece of software running in the background) creates notifications for her colleagues across the world. Next, she uses a service called Planet Explorer to look up on a map and mark an area of land. By the time she joins her team in Washington D.C. the next afternoon, a satellite will have scanned her area of interest, so she can see the changes that have occurred there, since she left Utrecht. She will have access to high-resolution images, color-corrected, and calibrated to accentuate the detail. Placed on top of a historical stack of over 500 images, the latest one produces a new layer of insight.

The train arrives at a platform at Schiphol. The station is right underneath the airport, making it easy for travelers, especially for those with children and luggage. As they step onto the platform, they give up the affordances of the train's environment, such as the seats and the Wi-Fi. They have access to a new set of things starting with the inclined moving walkway. As they emerge into the cavernous main hall of the airport, the ecosystem of services around them dramatically changes. Digital displays suggest which gates to go toward, retail stores suggest shopping, check-in kiosks suggest avoiding queues further inside, and the mere presence of the Koninklijke Marechaussee suggests you have entered a safe environment.[18]

Most services are a series of steps. Some of those steps are themselves services, producing a series of key outcomes that add up to some final outcome customers have in mind. Airports are an ecosystem of services that together facilitate the flow of passengers and bags through a series of performances and affordances. Several public and private enterprises work together to reduce the overall travel time for passengers while maintaining safety and security for all. Near Lounge 2 at Schiphol Airport, there is a section of the floor that is a glass ceiling. Through it you can see below the baggage handling system in action. By chance, you might even spot your own bag making its own 'hidden journey' to the gate. Several such journeys have to happen in the »back stage« for a single final outcome. These journeys run in parallel, intersecting at critical junctures which could end up being bottlenecks. European airports, airlines, and baggage handling companies are therefore exploring ways to improve the flow of passengers and bags. One of the ideas being tested is to allow passengers and their bags to travel separately from door-to-door, entirely bypassing the regular pathways through the airport.[19]

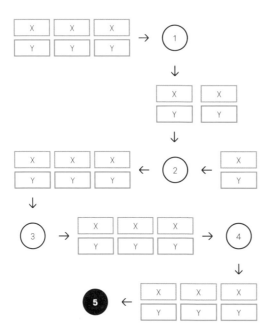

Figure 7
Series of outcomes,
Several journeys in parallel
leading to a final outcome

☐ Affordance (X)
☐ Performance (Y)

○ **Key outcome**
1 At the Airport
2 Checked-in
3 Boarding
4 Flying

● **Final outcome**
5 Walking on sunshine

It is time to check in for the flight. Alice is flying non-stop with KLM. She has already paid for the baggage allowance as part of her ticket purchase. She now arranges for her bags to be checked – the ones too large for the overhead cabin and those containing items restricted to the aircraft's hold.[20] She approaches the next available agent and initiates dialog and interaction. The agent turns out to be smart, helpful, and fully-automated – smart, dutiful, and tireless machines capable of directly interacting with passengers, checking IDs, looking up airline records, administering the security questionnaire, weighing the bags, printing boarding passes, issuing tags, and then placing the checked luggage on the moving conveyor belt behind them. Alice is not someone who is easily impressed. In this case she is.

Alice's bags are artifacts. Baggage handling is a series of performances: transporting, screening, sorting, diverting, and loading the bags, until they are in the aircraft's hold. The airline's information system adds bags to Alice's passenger name record and generates bag tags that serve as unique identifiers or »license plates«. The bags become identifiable and therefore ready for screening, sorting, and transporting.

Figure 8
Flows,
Series of performances,
affordances and outcomes

Affordance (X) ——
Performance (Y) ——
Key outcome   □
Final outcome   ■

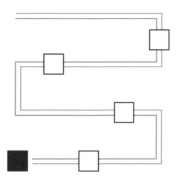

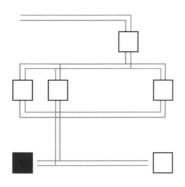

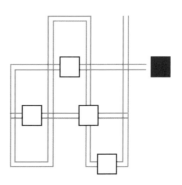

The system that generates bag tags is based on the IATA standard airlines and airports follow worldwide. Each bag tag has a 10-digit numeric code that uniquely identifies the bag and links it to the passenger and flight. That makes the entire set of billions of possible values (»address space«) an intangible industry resource, an instance of which is made available to a bag in the tangible form of a bar code.[21] *Alice's bags are events*. Baggage handling is a series of affordances, starting with the tags and the moving conveyor belt behind the airline desks: assigning each bag its own tray, security clearance, passage through a secure channel, space on pallets, and manual labor to assist the loading of the bags into the aircraft's hold.

After check-in, passengers and their carry-on bags go through security checkpoints. Once their boarding passes and bag tags get stamped with an invisible »OK«, they proceed to the gates for the boarding process. More performances and affordances ahead. Passengers stow away their bags in overhead bins, place personal items in seat pockets, and settle down in their assigned seats. Meanwhile, ground services fuel the aircraft, stock it with supplies, load it with bags, inspect it, and prepare it for the next take-off and landing cycle. Soon the pilots will get permission for pushback, be given a runway assignment, and take-off clearance. The control tower coordinates the movement of aircraft, separating them from other traffic and giving each temporary access to a most valuable resource – *the crisscross of runways* built on a reclaimed piece of land in North Holland, bought from a farmer in 1916 for 55229,40 guilders.

After take-off, other capabilities and resources come into play, on the ground and in the air, through sector after sector of controlled airspace. During the 8-hour flight to Washington D.C., for Alice and her bags the Boeing 777-300ER aircraft is a capability and resource. Its General Electric GE90 turbofan engines are the largest and most powerful in the industry, giving over 300 seats a range of up to 8555 nautical miles. For the air traffic control centers that are tracking it and allocating airspace en route, it is an artifact and event. *As KL651 completes its descent and glides into the approach for landing on a runway, the wide-body »artifact and event« carrying 286 passengers has already been assigned gate at Dulles Airport*. It will land on runway 19R and taxi to the terminal where people and things patiently wait – marshallers, chokes, jet ways, pallets, unit load devices, bag loaders, wheelchairs, gate agents and other ground staff, waiting for the pilot to cut off the engines after pulling up to the gate. And passengers with carry-on bags.

The devil is in the details

Throughout Alice's journey, from the check-in at Utrecht Central Station to the check posts controlled by the U.S. Department of Homeland Security, the ecosystem of services around her changes. Services fade in and fade out as if according to a well-written script (there isn't). The transitions are smooth because of the arrangements in place. However, not every journey goes as smoothly – without any disruption, damage, or delay. Things do go wrong.

Every service is a system – an interconnected set of elements that is coherently organized in a way that achieves something. The least obvious part of the system, its function or purpose is often the most crucial determinant of the system's behavior (Meadows, 2008). The parts may be tangible, intangible, fixed or moving, including those that customers fail to bring, forget to return, or find difficult to handle. The design process needs to systematically identify all those parts, their dependencies, and interactions. However, since there aren't any physical laws, standards, or regulations governing the design of services, it is easy to end up defining some elements in great detail while entirely missing others. Tim Brown, a leading expert on design explains (Brown, 2012):

> »In traditional attempts to design a service, we 'script' the service, creating a 'user experience blueprint' that attempts to describe everything that will happen to the customer during the experience. For a hotel, for instance, this would include everything from what the lobby looks like to what the check-in service is like. Attention to all these details leads to a relatively complicated script, which makes us confident that we have covered all the bases. The problem is, even when we get these scripts right, it's amazing how often things go wrong.«

Idea generation can produce a lot of noisy detail. In the absence of any filtering mechanism or a constraining logic. The low sig-

TIME SLOTS
AT SCHIPHOL

nal-to-noise ratio of such output makes it difficult to find and sort ideas that lead to genuine breakthroughs, while filtering out those that seem exciting but later prove to be too flaky, costly, or risky to implement. General purpose methods combined with simplistic notions of what services are – popular concepts from consumer marketing, now deeply ingrained – make us pay more attention to some kinds of detail over others. As George Carter, a professor of geography at Johns Hopkins University, wrote in 1963 in The Baltimore Sun:

> »It is axiomatic that the eye sees only what the mind prepares it to see. The hunter sees the rabbit, the bird watcher the bird, and too many tourists see only the motels and gas stations.«

Add to that the illusion of explanatory depth. Since services are common and their use is widespread – we all have user experience – we feel 'confident that we have covered all the bases', even with superficial and superfluous detail. As psychologists Leonid Rozenblit and Frank Keil explain (Rozenblit & Keil, 2002):

> »Most people feel they understand the world with far greater detail, coherence, and depth than they really do.«

That is less likely to happen, for example, if what we are designing is a surgical instrument, a cryptographic algorithm, or a suspension bridge.

To avoid the kind of detail that 'leads to a relatively complicated script', it is better to first »establish the soul, the meaning, the why of a product early on, using thoughtful strategic design« (Olson, 2017). For that we need to pay attention to the language we use for 'thinking in services'. We also need to be able to see the concept of a service always as a whole – problem and solution – regardless of the level of abstraction, or the level of detail. That way, as we progressively elaborate a concept, there won't be any missing elements or parts, because at every level of elaboration – 1x, 2x, 4x, 16x – we are always looking at »the whole and its parts.«

Clarity in concept cleanses the devil in the details.

CL ──────────────────▶ AR

         ┌──▶ **IN CONCEPT**
         │

Y ◀────────────── I

3

Patterns

3

Patterns are useful for developing greater clarity in the concept of a service and a deeper understanding of why services are the way they are and what they can be. Using them we can systematically construct and deconstruct solutions, and be more creative when confronted with complex problems.

Patterns provide a certain type of facility and advantage, as design theorist Christopher Alexander found while studying towns, buildings, and constructions (Alexander, Ishikawa, & Silverstein, 1977):

> »*Each pattern describes a problem that occurs over and over again in our environment, and then describes the core of the solution to that problem, in such a way that you can use this solution a million times over, without ever doing it the same way twice.*«

What's true in urban planning is just as true in services. For example, *verifying-something*, *authorizing-something*, and *transferring-something* are patterns that are used in millions of instances. In fact, it would be far easier to develop a pattern language for services since every service can be framed as a set of performances and affordances formed out of four types of things, which the two sides bring.

To understand how a pattern language can be useful in designing services, we turn to Dave Hora, Research Manager at PlanGrid – a company that develops productivity solutions for the construction industry.

Netflix on AWS
By Dave Hora, Research
Manager, PlanGrid

Alexander's pattern language is a set of a 253 distinct patterns that when selected, sequenced, and applied appropriately, will lead to harmonious environments. A generalized insight of the approach is this: given a collection of aligned patterns – a coherent language – this limited set of problem-solutions can help create a near-infinite variety of well-adapted responses to need, based on the context of pattern use, and order in which the patterns are selected and applied. It is through experience of application and sensitivity to results that a collection of patterns can be considered a coherent »pattern language« for a given domain rather than just a set of pattern descriptions.

»Amazon Web Services offers reliable, scalable, and inexpensive cloud computing services. Free to join, pay only for what you use.«

»Amazon Web Services offers reliable, scalable, and inexpensive cloud computing services. Free to join, pay only for what you use.«

The Amazon Web Services (AWS) is a market leader in cloud computing services.[22] The AWS service offerings are an illustrative example of how a coherent set of services, across a number of scales, may come to fit together. By considering every AWS offering a service pattern, developers find new ways to connect, combine, extend, and align these services into higher-order services. The AWS catalog has several lines of service, including computing, storage, databases, networking, content delivery, analytics, security, identity, and machine learning.

Starting in 2008, Netflix, the world-leader in on-demand video, chose to run their growing operations on AWS infrastructure, to be able to dependably produce high-quality outcomes and experiences, for millions of concurrent viewers. No matter who is watching which video from where in the world and at what time, the video should immediately start playing, without delay, and keep playing, without interruption. It is all due to a coherent set of software service patterns working at many levels of scale, with clear interconnected arrangements. It is made possible by hundreds of services together fulfill the promise of a monthly subscription.[23]

A brief note on scale. When our own design intent sits with a higher-level outcome than »storing files« or »running a web application«, we consider these kinds of capabilities as service offerings at a »micro« level: meant to be combined to create higher order performances and affordances. In the software-defined world of AWS we find a rich set of service patterns, complementary to

MICRO

each other, at levels between the most fundamentally »micro« and the ultimate »macro« services.

Imagine you're building a company that serves video on-demand to millions of customers who get to choose from a vast catalog. You have your own data center »on premises«, which is expensive to maintain in-and-of-itself before considering on-site staff and has visible limits on space and ability to scale. You're finding it terribly expensive to keep buying and installing storage as your video library grows wild.[24] So perhaps find a pattern that may solve your problem:

»Provide access to storage, perform file transfers.«

»Provide access to storage, perform file transfers.«

Instead of building more servers, you select the AWS Simple Storage Service \[S3] service to handle storing your media: it's a well-developed instance of a pattern addressing your need. They provide the facility, physical computers, power, networking, and security (all built on a web of »micro« services fully concealed from you) while ensuring it all runs smoothly – you just upload the video. When users on your website need access to video, your database points them to the \[S3] service instead of local servers. It's fast, reliable, and the beauty of this service is that your storage is no longer bound by constraints of your own physical hardware. It also costs much less.

But now we imagine you have an outage in your local data center: the database machines crash. And when your database goes down you can no longer serve your customers – the video is there (in the \[S3] service), your website is there (still hosted at your data center), but you have no way to load user accounts or reference the video. So, to complement the work we've already done with storage, we look back to the AWS catalog, and find:

»Provide access to database, perform relational queries.«

»Provide access to database, perform relational queries.«

That would be the AWS Relational Database Service \[RDS]. Just like your video, you migrate your records to the [RDS] service and now your website on-premises looks up user accounts and video content locations in an [RDS] service and then serves your video from the [S3] service.

The heavy technical work (a sequenced application of patterns) pays off: your company gets big, experiencing hockey stick growth, and your in-house data center can't handle all the traffic. The website is crawling, and it is only getting worse. So (what else?) your problem leads you to search for another service: »Provide scalable access to secure computer instances and perform calculations (run web apps).« In the language of AWS, this is the Elastic Compute Cloud \[EC2]. Now you've rebuilt your entire data center on someone else's infrastructure. Customers going to your website are pointed to the \[EC2] service, which looks up their account in the \[RDS] service, which points them to their videos on the \[S3] service. It's all so fast, cheap, scalable.

Then, we imagine, a final near-disaster strikes. Your customers are all over the country, the world, and the tubes are getting clogged: video coming from the \[S3] data center is sluggish. It has to travel too far! Without hesitation you reach into Amazon's library of patterns, and, wonderfully enough, find:

»Provide access to proxy, perform caching and distribution.«

This is the AWS Content Delivery Network or \[CloudFront]. You apply the \[CloudFront] service to your existing infrastructure and somehow, it seems to eat your \[S3] service, wrapping itself entirely around the outside. So, you point your \[RDS] service to the \[CloudFront] service to serve video to your users, and then the magic happens. \[CloudFront] takes your video from \[S3] and moves it all over the world. Whenever a user tries to access video, \[CloudFront] points them to the closest \[S3] location where the video is available.[25]

And onward. AWS is an amazing collection of these service-pattern units of ability, each offering is designed to plug and play nicely with all of the others. These software service patterns are very clean cut and laid out in a well specified contract, the API and service level agreements. Facing, embracing, edging, extending – AWS services unlock new capabilities to be delivered as a microservice – a new offering to be further aligned, extended, and combined as far as you please.

Within AWS itself, we find services designed to help you manage services, services designed to automate the work of other services, and services that help your services talk to each other. Consider the services your software engineers are using to store

Figure 9
GB Seconds

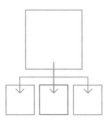

and manage their code that tells the AWS services what to do. And the services that help make any of it all work when computers connect to the internet. Taken together, the broad set of AWS solutions may be considered the living and coherent service pattern language of the world's largest cloud computing platform. A pattern language is meant to be a robust solution for a domain, encompassing all levels of scale. Alexander moves from the construction of window sills all the way to the nature of towns and regions. Similarly, for any set of services-in-use we can take a broader look and frame ‚microservices' as those that, from a given level of zoom, are a constituent part of a higher-level outcome. This simple pattern of relationship is not limited to a micro scale. Layers and networks of [micro]services, whether or not they come from a coherent language, are fused into full services offerings that create outcomes for customers. The same pattern moves upward to combine service capabilities into lines of service, lines of service into organizations, and organizations into markets and economies. It's all about your level of zoom, and the higher up you look, the more it is micro all the way down.

Might you, bakery-owner, use Uber to scaffold your local delivery offering? Then here, we consider it a microservice. Dentist, does Netflix on the ceiling make your practice a better experience? Then, for now, the service is micro. Do you, airline operator, require an outside organization to prepare and provide all of the food for your flights? From your point of view, their food-services organization is concealed as micro.

[Thank you Dave!]

Stereotypes

We can express the *why* of the service product using simple phrases characterizing a set of performances and affordances. Each phrase has two words. The first word of each phrase describes an *action* (the ing), and the second word describes a *thing*.

ing-thing[26]

analyzing-data
synchronizing-folder
tracking-object
updating-document

granting-permission
restoring-rights
leasing-equipment
dispensing-medicine

Each phrase characterizes one of the two aspects of a service: affordance and performance. In other words, there are two types of phrases corresponding to the two types of arrangements: type-X for affordance and type-Y for performance. Each X-Y pair is called a *stereotype*: a portmanteau of 'stereo' and 'type'. *Stereo-* as in more solid or stronger with two, and *-type* as in a characterization. One way to think of these stereotypes is looking through 3D glasses. Two separate prints become one solid image with clarity and depth. Stereotypes are minimalist expressions of service concepts, as the following examples illustrate.

In the first example, the stereotype characterizes services that give access to something based on the rights or privileges of an identity on record. For example, devices installed on doors and gates of buildings read ID cards and then open the door or gate. Officers at Schiphol examine Alice's passport and give (or deny) her permission to enter the secure area. In fact, citizens of certain countries can use the eGate, a self-service border checkpoint.

Examples of stereotypes

Y   verifying-identity
X   granting-permission

In this second example, the stereotype characterizes services that continuously track the current position of an object and then display or indicate its coordinates on a map or some other frame of reference. Once Alice's flight is in the air, radars along the entire route will track its position and let air traffic controllers know where it is at any given moment. In law enforcement, electronic bracelets do the same for those awaiting trial and whose movements are restricted by court orders.

X   indicating-coordinates
Y   tracking-object

This next example characterizes services that allow things to travel across a terrain or pass through an environment. For example, those tracks for the train that made Alice's 30-minute journey possible and the undersea cables through which terabytes of data per second flow between the United States and Europe, including Alice's file updates.

X   allowing-passage
Y   maintaining-velocity

More than one stereotype may be used to describe a concept. For example, we can describe a digital file storage service as follows:
1st pair
X   allocating-storage
Y   creating-copy

2nd pair
Y   synchronizing-folder
X   displaying-list

In many cases, one half of the stereotype is more obvious than the other. It requires further thought to recognize that pipes, cables, tracks, and air corridors help maintain velocity in terms of both speed and direction. The thinking that goes into framing a stereotype is important because of the implications for design. For example, when Alice goes through airport security, her bags will be screened to check if they contain anything that is dangerous or illegal.

Y   scanning-bags
X   granting-permission

Figure 10
Stereopsis

While Alice is quite sure her bags are clean and safe, they still need an »OK« or clearance from the security officer, without which she can't proceed with them further. That makes sense. But there are other stakeholders to consider, such as the airport, airline, and other passengers. From their perspectives, the service at the security checkpoints across the airport is providing the assurance that people and their possessions that pass through don't pose any threat. The outcome of *providing-assurance* (»This side of the airport is secure«) is a common good shared by all those stakeholders.

Y   scanning-bags
X   providing-assurance

THE BIG PICTURE

The performance of *scanning-bags*, (the outcome of which is, »We have looked inside them«) is thus paired with two separate types of affordances, to create two stereotypes that together characterize the service.

In some cases, within a stereotype or pair of arrangements, the artifact and the event are two separate things. The passport control gate at Schiphol scans Alice's passport (the artifact) and then grants her (the event) permission to go through. In other cases, the artifact and event are one and the same thing, as in the case of Alice's checked bags as they went through the baggage screening and sorting system. When Alice was herself passing through security, the body scanner was doing the screening (capability), and the officer was doing the granting, with a head nod and hand gesture (resource). The passport control gate, on the other hand, integrates capability and resource in one thing.

One could argue that the body scanner is the resource because of the affordance of the space in which Alice stands still for 10 seconds and is subject to millimeter waves. Therefore, for affordance, Alice is in an arrangement with the scanner. The counter-argument would be that the resource Alice needs is not necessarily the standing space but the permission. She could decline the millimeter wave, in which case security officers would use a hand-held scanner and a pat down. She would still need permission from someone or something who has the requisite authority. The scanner cannot give her that. It's the officer who does. Therefore, from an outcome perspective, for affordance, Alice (event) is in an arrangement with the officer's authority (resource). Whenever there is doubt as to which things form arrangements for performance or affordance, the clarification comes from asking the question: »What outcome is this pair expected to produce?«

When to stereotype

When improving the design of a service, it is sometimes useful to apply analogical reasoning and look into other domains that have similar problem structures. That way, one domain can examine underlying components such as skills, technologies, and methods, from another domain where they have proven themselves to be part of the solution. Looking inside bags at the airport is a lot like looking inside a patient to detect abnormalities and changes. Similar to the way that Alice specifies an area of interest for satellites to scan, neurologists, for example, specify dermatomes, or areas of a patient's anatomy with nerve endings that might be causing pain. Like Alice, they then wait for the results to arrive in the form of high-resolution images and layers of insight. It's possible then to pull up earlier records and to play back the changes. That's where the similarity ends. Alice is looking at pictures of the Earth's surface at a scale that's quite different from that of dermatomes or duffel bags. Airport security officers, on the other hand, actually look inside the bags, as do physicians, and they are in a position to decide if the bags are to be opened for further, more invasive examination. That's where that similarity ends.

Stereotypes are useful in defining microservices – services that are components from which other services can be built quickly, reliably, and elegantly. The scope of a microservice is a job that is fine-grained and frequently performed. When you are watching Netflix, for example, there may be a microservice running in the background that recognizes the device you will be watching on. Another may make sure video will be in the right format. One may maintain a list of movies and shows you have watched and liked, while another, equipped with Netflix's recommendation algorithm, takes that history to generate the list of suggestions. Netflix of course is a pioneer of the microservices architecture. Anecdotal evidence suggests, around 700 microservices independently running, together produce the macroservice also known as Netflix.

Spectrum

There are eight service patterns from which it is possible to develop new concepts. 1, 2, 3, and 4 show patterns in which capabilities and artifacts form performances. 5, 6, 7, and 8 show patterns in which resources and events form affordances. They are made available here using the same caveats and suggestions Alexander and others first offered their pattern language with: »these patterns are still hypotheses ... and are therefore all tentative, all free to evolve under the impact of new experience and observation.« They are also stated »... in a very general and abstract way – so that you can solve the problem for yourself, in your own way, by adapting it to your preferences, and the local conditions at the place where you are making it.« In that respect, the patterns presented here are basic and useful for framing and forming stereotypes, because they are general enough to be applied across service sectors, but still specific enough (about performances and affordances) to crystallize a concept.

Pattern 1 (EE)
Examine-Evaluate

EE-1

Capabilities examine a thing to form an idea or image of its condition or state, or to evaluate its worth. The value of the artifact increases merely from the new or additional information obtained; not just in the eyes of the owner but also in the eyes of others. Reducing fear, uncertainty, or doubt about the condition or state of the artifact may in effect increase its perceived value.

- Scanning a patient's anatomical detail to get insight into a health condition
- Appraising a piece of art to help buyers determine its market value
- Auditing financial statements to comply with regulations
- Analyzing credit card transactions to detect suspicious activity

Pattern 2 (MP)
Maintain-Protect

MP-2

Capabilities preserve the condition or state of a thing, or protect it from damage, disturbance, or disclosure. The value of the artifact increases with the length of time it continues to be the way it is. It also increases with any increase in the area or expanse within which it can be that way, or in the number of different places. Custodial care is part of the value proposition, as are low levels of ambient noise, disturbance, and interference.

- Maintaining a safety and privacy perimeter inside which guests can stay
- Archiving documents to maintain records of legal and financial transactions[27]
- Preserving biodiversity with seed samples from the world's crop collections[28]
- Maintaining a safe browsing session by blocking off phishing attempts

Pattern 3 (RR)
Restore-Repair

RR-3

Capabilities restore things to a previous condition or state or repair it from damage. The value comes from the artifact recovering or returning to its former self and resuming its role as an asset; with few or no signs of damage. The sooner the recovery, the greater the avoided loss from the asset being idle or impaired. The recovery is ideally stable and without stress. For example:

- Cleaning and sterilization of hospital linen
- Restoring data from a back-up after a major disaster

- Restoring the rights of a person through a judicial process
- Removing garbage from streets and homes

Capabilities transform things to more valuable conditions or states, or translate them to form new ideas or images. These transformations may be irreversible, or permanent. The translations create new artifacts that are themselves valuable. The value may depend not so much on the degree of difficulty but how profound the change.

- Converting a bank balance into a payment authorization or currency notes
- Issuing a passport or a national identity card based on a birth certificate
- Placing a satellite into a geosynchronous stationary orbit
- Executing instructions in a piece of software code[29]

Pattern 4 (TT)
Transform-Translate

TT-4

The resource allows things to enter, pass through it, and exit within a certain timeframe, to travel from one place to another. By maintaining entry and exit points at particular points, and adequate capacity in between, the resource affords the event the necessary passage. In effect, the resource connects or conducts the event. For the event, the value of the passage depends on criteria such as how far, how quickly, and how sure it can travel between two points, unhindered and uninterrupted. The events are *traffic*.[30]

- Transmitting terabytes of data per second between two continents[31]
- Allowing aircraft to safely fly through an air corridor along a particular route[32]
- Conveying a pouch of documents through a diplomatic channel[33]
- Distributing electricity to several neighborhoods

Pattern 5 (CC)
Conduct–Connect

CC-5

The resource allows things to occupy or stay for a duration of time, by being a conducive environment or container for the event. The arrival, stay, and departure define the affordance cycle, and the value comes primarily from having carrying capacity available at a particular place and time. In effect, the resource hosts the event. The events are *tenants*.[34]

Pattern 6 (CH)
Contain-Hold

CH-6

- Storage server holding a cache of digital content
- A hotel room accommodating the visit of a guest
- A safety deposit box keeping valuable contents
- Seed vault in the permafrost storing seed samples

Pattern 7 (LR)
Lease-Rent

Events borrow a resource, make use of it for a period of time, and then return it. During that period, the event has a fair degree of flexibility and control over the use of the resource. The value for the event comes from being able to treat the resource as a temporary asset, without the costs and risks associated with full ownership. The resource itself may depreciate from use during the period, but it is to be returned intact or free of damage.[35]

- Renting out vehicles or equipment for shortterm use
- Leasing commercial real estate for a business operation
- Lending money to be paid back with interest
- Renting artwork

Pattern 8 (DD)
Display-Dispense

The event acquires the resource for good and as a good. Returns are neither necessary, nor may they be possible when the resource is fully absorbed or consumed. Depending on the nature of the resource, it may be dispensed or distributed in portions, packages or units, or simply be projected or displayed for viewing. The mere presence of the resource in the vicinity or environment is good enough to satisfy the need. The resource may be publicly provisioned, for entire groups at a time, or given in private to specific groups or individuals.[36]

- Supplying electricity through a socket
- Dispensing food or drink from a vending machine
- Playing or projecting music and video to speakers and screens
- Granting status, privilege, or permission at a point of access

The eight patterns form a spectrum. The bands 1-4 represent degrees of performance. The bands 5-8 represent degrees of affordance (Davis & Chouinard, 2016). For example, recovering an online service taken down by a malicious attack (RR-3) is an additional degree of undertaking than simply defending it (MP-2). Similarly, renting an apartment (LR-7) is a higher degree of undertaking than simply staying at a hotel (CH-6). The degrees do not signify greater importance or difficulty. They are simply useful in formulating policy and strategy (e.g., in exploring adjacent market spaces: RR-3 to TT-4), and in identifying all the costs and risks that are general implications during the design, development, and implementation of a service (e.g., selling subscriptions to a movie catalog, DD-8, from offering video rentals, LR-7). The differences make sense only within a market space. For example, it may be far costlier and riskier to operate facilities that remove biohazard from hospital linen (RR-3) than to run virtual machines that promptly execute software code (TT-4).

The eight patterns also provide starting points or footholds from where to begin an inquiry, knowing that two of the eight patterns are the correct answers. So, when one of them is obvious (say it is pattern number 5, or CC), it helps us figure out the other (which now can only be 1, 2, 3, or 4). For example, the obvious pattern in a service that provides tracks for trains is number 5 (allowing-passage). Now, since we need two to complete a stereotype, which is the other one? What does the track do to the train in terms of performance? By the process of elimination, we arrive at pattern number 2 (MP) because »maintain its course and keep it going« is what the tracks do. More specifically, »maintain velocity«, because of the way tracks are designed, firmly fixed, leveled, and then laid out with stretches and curvatures that form the route.

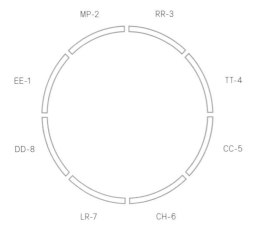

Figure 11
Spectrum of possibilities

☐ Performance (Y)
☐ Affordance (X)

The eight patterns help us to more systematically frame stereotypes, to construct and deconstruct service concepts, some-

Analytical rigor

times forcing us to think deeper than we normally would, to be able to explain the phenomenon of a service. They help us challenge ideas and assumptions and get in the way of popular notions. In 2015, the following piece of punditry, heralding a new wave of disruption, made several rounds of the Internet:

»Uber, the world's largest taxi company, owns no vehicles. Facebook, the world's most popular media owner, creates no content. Alibaba, the most valuable retailer, has no inventory. And Airbnb, the world's largest accommodation provider, owns no real estate. Something interesting is happening.« (Goodwin, 2015)

Tom   No, they don't, and therefore they are not.

[Uh oh! They're are back.]

Jerry   You cannot be a taxi company without a fleet of vehicles, or drivers. By vehicle I mean a container or enclosed space that is capable of producing controlled movement or conveyance, changing the physical coordinates of the things it is moving, to eventually coincide with those of the destination.

Tom   Patterns 4 and 6.

Jerry   The transportation formula. Don't know why the commissioners in California ruled otherwise.

Tom   Something about Uber exercising extensive control over its drivers. Still, the fact is that Uber is as much a taxi company as travel companies like Priceline, Expedia and Kayak are airlines.

Jerry   It will be a taxi company if and when it deploys a fleet of autonomous vehicles with software drivers. Right now it is primarily a platform that matches drivers with passengers. The matchmaking model based on patterns 4 and 8.

Tom   And so much for Airbnb disrupting the hotel industry. Apparently, 2017 was the best year ever for hotel occupancy in the United States. Marriott and Hilton stocks are both up more than 40 percent in the last 12 months (Thompson, 2018).

Jerry   The 2-6 combination is time tested. The hospitality formula. Hotels don't just offer a nice place to stay. They also maintain a perimeter within which there is a certain level of safety, security, and caretaking. They have

housekeeping staff who maintain cleanliness and comfort within a room, throughout the stay. Airbnb hosts
might be helpful, giving you a warm welcome, and a lot
of useful local advice. But they do that as innkeepers, not
Airbnb.

Tom   Oh yeah. Feeling carefree – not having to worry too much
about making a mess – is part of the affordance.

Tom   And, in Berlin, if someone catches you entering the hotel, you don't have to pretend you are friends of the hotel
manager [Laughs]. Airbnb stays do offer some amazing
opportunities though. Some of the homes are at these
most wonderful locations where you won't find any hotels. Plus, you get to live as the locals do.

[Ok guys, thank you for chiming in.]

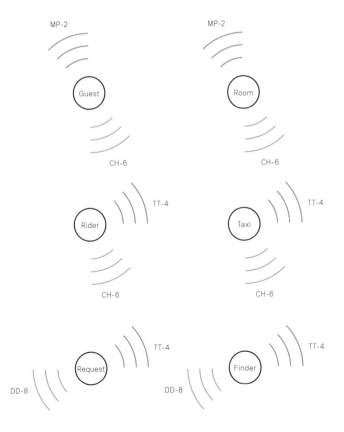

Figure 12
Transportation, hospitality
and matchmaking

Forecasting demand is an important part of designing a service. If we were to look at sources of demand and study them both as artifacts and events, we may find they generate demand in more or less fixed patterns because they are going through a procedural sequence. This kind of analysis is valuable in designing systems in which demand is handed off from one service to another, as in the case of baggage handling.

Figure 13
Forecasting

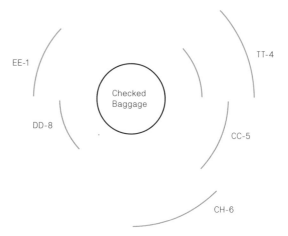

A coordinating entity has to manage the hand-offs to ensure a smooth journey through the system. Each pattern of demand comes with its own type of costs and risks, modes of failure, and therefore forecast requirements – heads up! This is particularly important in systems that involve several providers, each responsible for a key outcome. They all have to do their part well for the system to produce the final outcome. To be coordinated they have to share information – e.g., coordinated care for patients, baggage handling, and processing a request for asylum.

Part

Two

4

Promises

4

Services are arrangements and agreements – agreements between people and arrangements between things. The arrangements are necessary for performances and affordances »to happen.« The agreements are necessary for the arrangements »to take place.«

Capabilities and artifacts define performances. Resources and events define affordances. Customers and service providers define outcomes. Users and agents define experiences. Several arrangements and agreements come together to support a single customer journey. Some of them are more visible than others. The potential for services exists between any two things. Performances and affordances may be waiting to happen. But that doesn't mean they are going to happen, or even allowed to happen. How good the arrangements are affects performances and affordances, and therefore the quality of outcomes and experiences. If the arrangements aren't properly made, the service fails to meet expectations. There needs to be clear and complete agreement between people on both sides of the arrangements – customers and service providers.

Figure 14
People and things

Affordance (X) ———
Performance (Y) ———

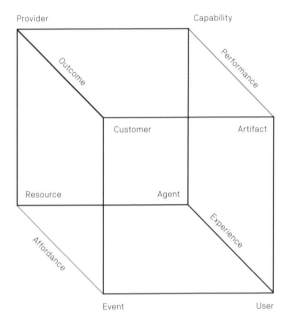

Figure 14
People and things

Affordance (X) ———
Performance (Y) ———

Ephemeral band

During Alice's 30-minute journey earlier that morning, and we're simplifying here for the sake of illustration, the train was part of three major arrangements: with the tracks underneath, with the cables overhead, and with broadband networks. The arrangements were in place because of the agreements the train operator, the Nederlandse Spoorwegen (NS) has with ProRail – for the tracks, with Eneco – for the electricity, and with Nomad Digital – for the Wi-Fi network. By integrating cellular networks, trackside Wi-MAX networks, and a wireless client bridge between the train and the station, Nomad sets up a single and continuous broadband connection, for passengers to use throughout their journey.

Just before boarding the train, as part of an agreement, Alice placed her OV-chipkaart in close proximity to the card reader on one of the many gates and posts (poortjes en paaltjes). That brief hand gesture was the physical arrangement through which her card was loaded with a valid fare. With it came user privileges for the Wi-Fi connection. A dialog box pops up when you try to join the train's Wi-Fi network, presenting the terms and conditions for the use of the Wi-Fi. Accepting that agreement allows Alice's phone and the Wi-Fi routers on the train to form an arrangement in the form of a broadband connection, which Alice can now treat as a temporary asset, and use to connect to other services.

The Spotify app has access to the phone's hardware, to form an arrangement through which the daily mix can endlessly play. If a song on the mix isn't already on the phone, the app connects to Spotify's servers, and receives more songs, making use of Alice's Wi-Fi connection. Spotify's licensing agreements with copyright owners allow that arrangement to take place. Similarly, since Dropbox has Alice's permission, as part of its terms of use, to use the Wi-Fi connection to send and receive data, every time it detects changes. *Meanwhile over 150 satellites are line-scanning the Earth. Together they cover the entire landmass of the planet every single day. One of them will form arrangements with the area of interest Alice has earlier marked.*

Alice got a lot done during that ride to the airport, taking care of some work and taking care of herself. On one hand, there is nothing extraordinary about the train ride itself. Thousands of such journeys happen every day. Alice could have been sipping juice, ordering books, and enjoying the landscape instead – with windmills, cows, and the canal alongside.[37] What is extraordinary is how several services come into play to support the journeys. *Five services together form a continuous ephemeral band that is Alice's 30-minute journey: the railway tracks, the electricity, the broadband connection, a double-decker row of seats, and song tracks playing.* The money Alice spent that ticket pays off gradually every inch of the way (or centimeter should we say?).

Service agreements come in many formats. A ticket stub from a cinema vending machine, valid for a show later that day, is as much an agreement as one that may span a few hundred pages, valid for the next few years. Some agreements have a lot of fine print. Customers rarely ever read that, but nevertheless accept it by scrolling down, checking a box, and clicking a button. Others are unwritten contracts between citizens and governments. The formats of agreements vary a lot depending on the kind of service because of the people and things they cover. The differences exist for many reasons, including the rules, regulations, legacies and norms that are in force in certain societies, industry sectors, and markets. Also, because of the costs and risks involved.[38]

Service agreements

But here, we're interested in the similarities more than the differ-ences, to define the skeletal structure of a service agreement. A structure simple enough for the underlying design to be im-plemented with just a few lines of code (for example, as smart contracts on the Ethereum network), or the »few thousand lines« that may be necessary for business process outsourcing. It should make sense for microservices just as much as to Mainte-nance, Repair and Overhaul (MRO). Ambitious we are, aren't we? And why not? We have already put in the work. We have estab-lished the conceptual basis for it. Now we just need to »see« it.

Agreements are based on promises. Services require agree-ments, therefore services are also based on promises. But how do promises relate to the core concepts of a service? How do they represent performance, affordance, demand, and supply? What promises do service providers make? What do customers promise in return?

The idea of a promise

According to The Collins English Dictionary, a promise is an un-dertaking or assurance given by one person to another, agree-ing or guaranteeing to do or give something, or not to do or give something, in the future. Customers and service providers un-dertake to bring things to the arrangements. In doing so they to-gether assure that performances and affordances will take place in ways necessary to produce the outcomes (and experiences) that fulfill needs. While service providers assure the fulfillment of needs, customers assure payments. To do something relates to performance. To give something relates to affordance.[39]

According to The Oxford English Dictionary, a promise is a decla-ration or assurance that one will do something or that a particular thing will happen; an indication that something is likely to occur. The key words in that definition are declaration, likely, happen, and occur. Declarations make the motivations and expectations of one side clear to the other, and less vague. Since we have two sides participating in performances and affordances, it should be clear what each side is motivated to offer, and what they ex-pect in return. Even in the simplest of services there is uncertain-ty and risk. Even trains, for example, can't take the electricity and tracks for granted. Until they actually happen, performances and affordances are likelihoods.

According to Mark Burgess, a physicist and an expert on the design of systems based on cooperation, promises are: expressions of intent made by autonomous agents that are voluntary in nature, can be rejected by whom they're offered to, and cannot be impositions (Burgess, 2015).

So are services. Customers express their intent to participate in performances and affordances by having things that habitually suffer shortcomings and shortfalls. They are showing their propensity for services. For example, by paying taxes, signing up for subscriptions, and incorporating absent assets in the »scheme of things«, customers are effectively promising demand. Service providers respond to propensity with audacity. They invest in capabilities and resources, employ agents, and publish schedules, menus, and prices that promise supply. Their promises have to be bold to encourage customers to depend on them for performances and affordances. Propensities and audacities find themselves in feedback loops.

You cannot force someone to pay for or make use of a service, or to facilitate or provide one. Some services seem forced upon (or »not optional«), such as those required by law or membership in groups, societies, and organizations. Paying for or making use of a service may be a condition for participation. Therefore, while being required to go through a financial audit, a certification, or a background check, for example, may not seem voluntary, it actually is.

With that set up, let's open the doors of perception. A few sips of an adult beverage are now recommended.

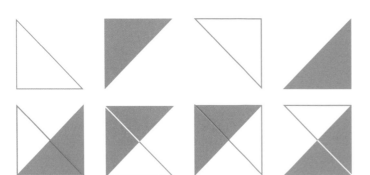

Figure 15
Venn diagrams

☐ X
■ -
☐ Y
■ +

**The four
promises**

Services are a set of promises. Four promises, *demand for affordance* [X -], *supply for affordance* [X +], *demand for performance* [Y -], and *supply for performance* [Y +] – corresponding to the four types of things. Two of the promises are from the demand side and two from supply. Two are for performance and two for affordance. The four promises frame the concept of a service. This framing is also known as the *4x frame*.

Figure 16
Gestalt of services

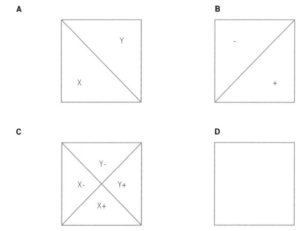

A   Performance and affordance are the two *aspects* of service. The diagonal separating them is the *line of action* – all action happens along its direction.

B   Demand and supply are the two *sides* of a service. This diagonal is the *line of interaction* – all dialog and interaction between the two sides happens across this line.

C   Each side covers both aspects. Each aspect includes both sides. Half of each side is for one aspect; the other half for the other aspect. The sides and aspects intersect to define four parts that make a service whole.

D   The service as »a whole that is other than the sum of its parts.« (Kurt Koffka) i.e., the service that emerges from the combination of the four promises has its own properties that do not exist within the parts themselves.

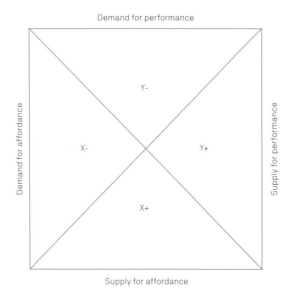

Figure 17
The 4x frame

	[-] Demand for	[+] Supply for
[Y] Performance	Y -	Y +
[X] Affordance	X -	X +

Each promise can be independently conceived, conceptualized, or thought of but you always need two to define performance [Y + and X +], affordance [X + and X -], demand [Y - and X -], and supply [Y + and X +]. Two adjacent promises form a side or an aspect. One side by itself cannot promise either performance or affordance. Commitments are required from both sides.

Customers and service providers make 'promising' statements to encourage each other with demand and supply. Propensity matches audacity, and vice versa. When promises are kept by both sides, there is accumulation of goodwill and trust. Both sides are then willing to take more risks, because, as the credibility of claims goes up, the costs go down.

Promising statements

Let's look at a few formats, with examples.

Promise statements can simply be 'classifieds' in a market space.

I promise [Y -].
I promise [X -].

In response to:
I promise [Y +].
I promise [X +].

I promise [*a method for appraising art*].
I promise [*the credibility for issuing authoritative opinions*].

In response to:
I promise [*art that needs to be appraised*].
I promise [*an estate sale that needs to have prices*].

For each promise there is a counter promise from the other side. Promises of demand [Y - or X -] are offered in return for (or accepted as a consideration toward) promises of supply [Y + or X +]. In other words, X + and X - are reciprocal to each other, as are Y + and Y -.

I promise [Y -], if you promise [Y +].
I promise [Y +], if you promise [Y -].

I promise [X -], if you promise [X +].
I promise [X +], if you promise [X -].

I promise [*an engine that needs to be tuned*], if you promise [*the skills and equipment*].
I promise [*the skills and equipment*], if you promise [*an engine that needs to be tuned*].

I promise [*brakes that need to have new linings*], if you promise [*original parts and certified labor*].
I promise to have [*original parts and certified labor*], if you promise to have [*brakes that need to have new linings*].

This is important for service agreements to form valid contracts, which, at a minimum, require an offer, a consideration, and acceptance.

The promises may coincide with each other. This means that when customers are promising demand for affordance (X -), they are also promising demand for performance (Y -), and vice versa. Similarly, when providers are promising supply for affordance (X +), they are also promising supply for performance (Y +) with it, and vice versa. A promise for performance may be secondary to the promise for affordance, or vice versa.

I promise [Y -], as well as [X -].
I promise [X -], as well as [Y -].

I promise [Y +], as well as [X +].
I promise [X +], as well as [Y +].

I promise [*soiled linen that needs to be cleaned*], as well as [*empty closets that need to have linen*].
I promise [*empty closets that need to have linen*], as well as [*soiled linen that needs to be cleaned*].

I promise [*cleaning and sterilization of linen*], as well as [*delivery carts stacked with clean linen*].
I promise [*delivery carts stacked with clean linen*], as well as [*cleaning and sterilization of linen*].

Promises may be demanded as collateral.

When you promise [Y -], you must also promise [X -].
When you promise [Y -], you must also promise [X -].

When you promise [*a card that needs to have a boarding fare*], you must also promise [*an account balance that needs to be debited*].

When you promise [*debiting of my account balance*], you must also promise [*the loading of my card with the boarding fare*].

Figure 18
Promise statements

Classifieds **A**
Counters **B**
Combinations **C**
Collateral **D**

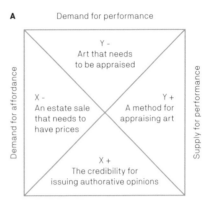

A

Demand for performance

Demand for affordance

Supply for performance

Y –
Art that needs
to be appraised

X –
An estate sale
that needs to
have prices

Y +
A method for
appraising art

X +
The credibility for
issuing authorative opinions

Supply for affordance

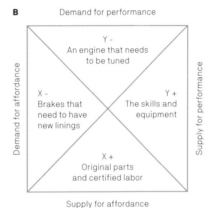

B

Demand for performance

Demand for affordance

Supply for performance

Y –
An engine that needs
to be tuned

X –
Brakes that
need to have
new linings

Y +
The skills and
equipment

X +
Original parts
and certified labor

Supply for affordance

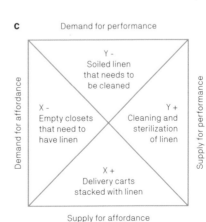

C

Demand for performance

Demand for affordance

Supply for performance

Y –
Soiled linen
that needs to
be cleaned

X –
Empty closets
that need to
have linen

Y +
Cleaning and
sterilization
of linen

X +
Delivery carts
stacked with linen

Supply for affordance

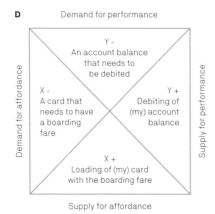

It is possible to create new and interesting 4x frames by exploring various combinations of the four types of promises. Each new 4x frame simultaneously explores the problem and solution. Changes to any one of the four promises in a 4x frame might prompt a reframing of the entire concept. Let's illustrate this idea with a word game. Imagine four bins marked X-, X+, Y- and Y+. Each bin contains a number of generic promises of that type. Then, it should be possible to combine random picks into a set of four promises that form a valid concept.

A   Something that needs to have its own space
           Something that needs to have replenishment
           Something that needs to have assurance
           Something that needs to have awareness

B   Something that needs to be elsewhere
           Something that needs to be repaired
           Something that needs to be bought or sold
           Something that needs to be translated

C   Issuing an authorative opinion or judgment
           Carrying things for a period of time
           Renting things for use
           Allowing passage

D   Detecting moving objects
           Making fair and accurate assessments
           Animating things into exciting states
           Isolating things from environments

New combinations

Figure 19
Four bins

A
X-

B
Y-

C
X+

D
Y+

[Y -] + [Y +] & [X -] + [X +] = valid concept?

Frame #1
Something that needs to be repaired is combined with the ability for making fair and accurate assessments. What's the point
of making fair and accurate assessments if others aren't willing
to accept the results? Therefore, the ability to issue an authoritative opinion or judgment seems complementary here. What
»need to have« do we combine it with? Something that needs to
have what? Its own space, replenishment, assurance, or awareness? When do things that need to be repaired benefit also from
a fair and accurate assessment? Two scenarios or situations
come to mind. (1) When a vehicle has suffered damage in an ac-
cident, and the owner files an insurance claim. The insurance
company sends someone with the knowledge, skills, and experience to investigate accidents and assess damage. (2) When a
court or commission finds someone to have actually suffered
injustice, wrongdoing, fraud, or abuse, there can be disputes or
challenges about what reparations they should receive. In both
cases, there is something that needs to have a compensation
or award that covers the losses. That requires fair estimates.
Therefore, assurance comes close, but only to the extent that
the estimates are in fact assurances of objectivity, fairness, and
transparency.

Therefore, the combination of [Something that needs to be re-
paired] + [Making fair and accurate assessments] & [Something
that needs to have assurance] + [Issuing an authoritative opinion
or judgment], is a valid concept.

Frame #2
Let's say we replace something that needs to have assurance
with something that needs to have awareness. Awareness of
what or in what situation? Can that awareness come from something that provides an authoritative judgment or opinion? Given
our random picks, that depends on whether we also have something that needs to be repaired, be elsewhere, be bought or sold,
or be translated. Perhaps someone or something has the need
to be elsewhere, which is why they need situational awareness.
They need GPS coordinates perhaps? We look at the picks from
the Y+ bin. It could be that detecting moving objects fits the bill
in this. Making fair and accurate assessments could be a part of
the promise.

Therefore, the combination of [Something that needs to be else-where] + [Detecting moving objects] & [Something that needs to have awareness] + [Issuing an authoritative opinion or judgment], is a valid concept. However, »Issuing an authoritative opinion« now sounds like a vague promise. So, let's change it to »Display-ing current coordinates«.

What practical value can a word game like this have? Customers with a new problem to solve may turn to services for a solution. Before jumping to conclusions about which service can solve it, it is useful to generate a few 4x frames, to explore ideas in the abstract form, achieve clarity, and then see which services out there might best complete the frame. Customers would hold the »minuses« constant, and cycle or flip through a set of »pluses« until they have the most compelling frame. Service providers make similar explorations, by doing the opposite: holding the »pluses« constant and varying the »minuse« to generate new 4x frames. Providers are exploring the problem space to discover new opportunities they otherwise wouldn't have thought of.

The combined effect of the four promises is an intangible prod-uct – *a particular set of outcomes and experiences at a par-ticular price.* Any of the four promises can improve the quality of this product. By the same token, the product fails to materialize when any one of the promises isn't kept.

Factorial design

The way the promises relate to each other makes it a complex product. By complex we mean depending on the values of several factors and that factors interact in a non-linear fashion. If you pay close attention to the Venn diagrams, the promises are inter-locked (like the bottom flaps of a cardboard box). The promises can strengthen or weaken each other through positive (reinforc-ing) feedback loops.[40]

»The more/less you promise [Y -], the more/less I promise [Y +]. The more/less I promise [Y +] the more/less I promise [X +]. The more/less I promise [X +], the more/less you promise [X -]. The more/less you promise [X -], the more/less I can promise [Y -].« Failing to account for the presence and influence of feedback loops are why many service improvement efforts fail; aside from the explorations being one-dimensional or one-factor-at-a-time. Such improvements turn out to be superficial, short-lived, and even counterproductive; creating new problems and commissioning a mindless number of iterations. A better approach is to follow the principles of factorial design and design of experiments, to understand within a few trials the effects of several different factors on the quality of the complex product.

Here is what Simon says about the architecture of complexity:

»Complexity frequently takes the form of hierarchy ... Hierarchic systems evolve far quicker than non-hierarchic systems of comparable size ... Hierarchy is one of the central structural schemes that the architect of complexity uses.«

As we shall see, service design is factorial design-friendly. Each of the four promises is the combined effect of four factors – *who, why, how* and *what* – giving us *16 questions* to inquire about the nature of the complex product. Each factor can be assigned values. Changes to the factors cause the promises to change. Changes to the promises cause the complex product to change. The product, promises, factors, and parameters and their causal relationships form the hierarchic structure of services that we can visualize with a cause-and-effect diagram.

Figure 20
Hierarchic structure

Factors →
X →
Y →

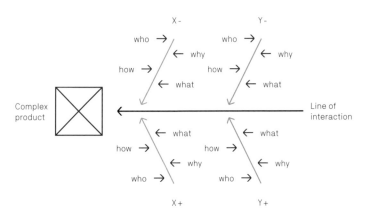

A new format

While cause-and-effect diagrams have a simple easy-to-draw format that readily shows the hierarchic structure of services, we need a special format for services – a data structure that encodes the design logic of services (the interlocking sides,

»Complexity frequently
takes the form of hierarchy ...

Hierarchic systems evolve
far quicker than non-hierarchic systems of comparable
size ...

Hierarchy is one of the
central structural schemes
that the architect of complexity uses.«

—

Herbert Alexander Simon

aspects, and promises); facilitates recording the answers from the 16 questions and cross-checking them for gaps and conflicts; prevents the illusion of explanatory depth; filters the kind of noisy detail that 'leads to a relatively complicated script'; and allows to simultaneously think about the problem and solution. Why should we impose so many design constraints on this new format? Because we are often asked to design complex products that solve complex problems.

In his book, *Frame Innovation: Create New Thinking by Design* (2015), Kees Dorst describes problems that are so open, complex, dynamic, and networked that they seem impervious to solution. Open problems lack clear boundaries; complex ones deal with the interconnectedness of several elements, with small changes in any one element changing the system as a whole; changing situations and shifting connections make problems dynamic; and, in increasingly networked societies, problems shape and influence each other. Together the four properties frustrate conventional approaches to problem solving based on decomposing simplistic models of the problem into subproblems, analyzing them, developing solutions, and then putting those together to solve the overall problem.

Dorst might very well be describing the challenges of designing services. Services are solutions that can be more difficult to design than a manufactured product of equivalent value. Part of it has to do with services being problems that are too open, complex, and dynamic. The rest of it has to do with how we frame the concept of a service, both, as a problem and a solution. We cannot think about solutions before truly understanding the problem. We cannot truly understand a problem without first imagining solutions. Therefore, we have to form bridges between problem spaces and solutions spaces, alternating between the two, and iterating until each becomes clearer and more refined from the other (Dorst & Cross, 2001).

That is why we need the special format. In the form of a grid – a structure common across many disciplines. Keeping in mind the »architecture of complexity« as per the »last Renaissance man«, it is a *simple hierarchic grid*. Let us see what this grid looks like, and feels like, by using it to understand the four factors that define the four promises.[41]

–	–	–	**+ –**
–	–	**+ –**	+
–	**+ –**	+	+
+ –	+	+	+

XY	Y	Y	**YY**
X	XY	**YY**	Y
X	**XX**	XY	Y
XX	X	X	XY

1	2	3	**4**
2	1	**4**	3
3	**4**	1	2
4	3	2	1

who	why	how	**what**
why	who	**what**	how
how	**what**	who	why
what	how	why	who

Figure 21
Simple hierarchic grid

5

Factors

5

1 Who is making the promise?
2 Why are they willing to?
3 How will they keep it?
4 What are they promising?

Four factors

The four factors are: who, why, how, and what.

Who (1) and *why* (2) describe the motivations of the side making a promise. *How* (3) and *what* (4) describe the expectations for the side accepting it. The motivations on each side set the expectations on the other. The promises are reciprocal. In making their promises, each side has to think about the benefits for the other. This way, both sides are equal stakeholders in the service. *Why* and *how* (2 and 3) define arrangements between things. *Who* and *what* (1 and 4) define agreements between people. The combination (1, 2, 3 and 4) creates the complex product – a particular set of outcomes and experiences at a particular price.

Let's further understand the four factors by using them to make sense of a real-life case – that of a hospital procuring the services of a commercial laundry for the cleaning and sterilization of its linen. Our approach will be to go through the »story« and mark up sentences and phrases with the four factors: who, why, how, and what. We will place the marked-up text on a 4x4 grid with that encodes the logic of sides, aspects, and promises. Its 16 panels afford us the space we need to store the information we extract from the case – *16 answers from the four questions we repeat across the four promises.* Each panel on the grid has a number and a label. The numbers indicate the sequence in which here we ask the four questions. Later they take on a lot

more meaning. The label is of the format: ⟨*factor=parameter*⟩.
The four factors are common across the four promises; the parameters are specific to each.

Figure 22
Deriving the four factors

A
A promise as a *whole*

B
Expectation □
Motivation ■

C
Arrangement □
Agreement ■

D
Experience □
Outcome ■

E
A+B+C+D=E

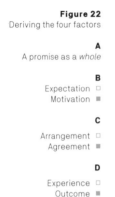

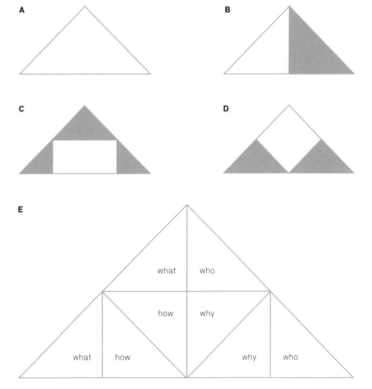

The labels function as tags similar to the ones used in mark-up
languages such as HTML, giving meaning to the bracketed content, as shown in the following four examples:

1 ⟨who = customer⟩   hospital directors are accountable for
                            the safety and comfort of care set-
                            tings. ⟨/who⟩

2 ⟨why = artifact⟩   linen such as gowns, towels, and
                            sheets for instance. ⟨/artifact⟩

3 \<how = task\>   needs to be carefully cleaned and
                          sterilized. \</how\>

4 \<what = enhancement\> hospitals agree to pay a fee simply for
                          converting soiled linen into fresh linen.   **Figure 23**
                          \</what\>   4x4

1 who = customer	2 why = artifact	3 how = task	4 what = enhancement
X -, Y -	Y -	Y -	Y +, Y -
2 why = event	1 who = user	4 what = commission	3 how = activity
X -	X -, Y -	Y +, Y -	Y +
3 how = access	4 what = provision	1 who = agent	2 why = capability
X -	X +, X -	X +, Y +	Y +
4 what = enrichment	3 how = availability	2 why = resource	1 who = provider
X +, X -	X +	X +	X +, Y +

In the first example, the text gets highlighted because it seems to provide an answer to the »question of who«. Therefore, we mark it up by enclosing it with the <who> </who> tags. Since we know in this case the hospital is the customer who promises to pay for the laundry service, we set the parameter to »customer«. Therefore, we use <who = customer> to mark the beginning of the highlighted text, and </who> to mark the end.

In the second example, the text tells us why a hospital is willing and able to promise the laundry work: linen gets heavily soiled on a daily basis. That is »why=artifact«. Which brings us to the third example, or how the hospital keeps its promise– in the form of a cleaning and sterilization »task« for the laundry to perform. The fourth state-ment indicates what the hospital is promising: a fee for the en-hancement of the artifact – the soiled linen cleaned and sterilized.

Factors	Parameters
who	customer, user, provider, agent
why	capability, resource, artifact, event
how	task, access, activity, availability
what	enhancement, enrichment, commission, provision

Case: Stacks, stocks, and flow

The linen is critical to the hospital's daily operations. Hospital staff and patients make use of linen, such as scrubs, gowns, and sheets, every single day. The linen becomes easily soiled from nor-mal use in a healthcare setting. It needs to be frequently changed to avoid infections, diseases and discomfort. We choose this case because it affords us the opportunity of understanding how the four factors separate the motivations of customers (the hos-pital's management) from those of the users (hospital staff), and those of the providers (the laundry's management) from those of the agents (laundry staff). At the same time, we need to see how the expectations from the two sides join together to form a set of outcomes and experiences.

Hospitals care about the safety and comfort of the settings in which patients receive care by physicians and nurses. Medical errors and infections are to be avoided at all costs.

Marked-up text

<who = customer> Hospitals are therefore willing to pay for the processing of soiled linen and adequate supplies of clean linen. </who> <who=user> Patients, physicians, nurses, and other staff, make daily use of linen </who> <why = artifact> such as gowns, towels, and sheets for instance. </why> The linen gets soiled from regular use. <how = task> It needs to be carefully cleaned and sterilized </how> to remove traces of blood and other fluids. <why = event> Staff then immediately need to have clean linen for patients and for themselves. </why> The longer the wait, the greater the risk of infections, diseases and discomfort. <how = access> Stacks of clean linen within easy reach of physicians and nurses, </how> improve the level of attention and care patients receive. On a normal day, the hospital generates large loads of soiled linen. Cleaning and sterilizing require <why = capability> a special process with a careful balance of chemicals, temperature, and pH levels. </why> This includes a 9-step computer-controlled process, to ensure that the clean linen does not cause skin irritation. Being able to handle such large loads requires <why = resource> industrial-scale equipment and large amounts of energy, water, chemicals, and detergents. </why> <who = provider> Providers specializing in processing linen for healthcare, </who> are expected to have such capabilities and resources, including a skilled workforce trained to work in an environment that includes the biohazard in hospital linen.

Hospital staff work long hours under stress. Therefore, the laundry deploys <who = agent> teams who take full responsibility for the soiled and clean linen. </who> Nurses can focus on the patients instead, and <what = commission> simply place soiled linen in bags and bins marked for the soiled closet. </what> The soiled closet is physically separate from the clean closet, to avoid cross-contamination. The laundry staff <what = commission> pick up the linen from the soiled closet </what> and transport it in trucks to the laundry facility. The linen then goes through a treatment process that includes <how = activity> sorting, washing,

4 WHAT

1 WHO

3 HOW

2 WHY

drying, inspection, ironing, and folding. </how> To assure an adequate and continuous supply of fresh linen, the laundry dedicates enough capacity in terms of <how = availability> machine cycles, work shifts, and trips to the hospital </how> that result in stacks of clean linen at the hospital. The laundry staff <what = provision> stack the linen in clean closets and exchange carts across the hospital. </what> <what = provision> That way the hospital staff can quickly grab what they need and be with patients. </what>

Since the provider serves several hospitals within an area, through economies of scale, they process the linen at a much lower cost. Therefore, they offer attractive pricing in return for a steady stream of demand. The hospital agrees to <what = enhancement> pay the laundry a management fee </what> for assuming the responsibility of <what = enhancement> converting soiled linen into clean linen. </what> The laundry finds that attractive because it covers their fixed costs, including maintaining their facility as if it were located inside each hospital. The laundry promises there will be <what=enrichment> an adequate stock of clean linen across the hospital at all times. </what> <what=enrichment For that, the hospital offers to pay a convenience fee per stack, </what> which goes toward the laundry's variable costs.

1 Who is making the promise?

A promise has to be credible. The first factor therefore is who is behind a promise. That helps whoever is considering accepting the promise to evaluate whether what is being promised is credible, and what they may have to offer in return. Customers and users are behind the promises of demand. Providers and agents are behind the promises of supply.

Figure 24
Step 1

<who = agent>   teams who take full responsibility for the soiled and clean linen. </who>

<who = provider>   providers specializing in processing linen for healthcare. </who>

<who = customer>   hospitals are willing to pay for the processing of soiled linen and adequate supplies of clean linen. </who>

----
1 who   2 why

<who = user>   patients, physicians, nurses, and other staff make daily use of linen. </who>

1 who = customer	2 why = artifact	3 how = task	4 what = enhancement
Hospitals are therefore willing to pay for the processing of soiled linen and adequate supplies of clean linen			
X -, Y -	Y -	Y -	Y +, Y -
2 why = event	1 who = user	4 what = commission	3 how = activity
	Patients, physicians, nurses, and other staff, make daily use of linen		
X -	X -, Y -	Y +, Y -	Y +
3 how = access	4 what = provision	1 who = agent	2 why = capability
		Teams who take full responsibility for the soiled and clean linen	
X -	X +, X -	X +, Y +	Y +
4 what = enrichment	3 how = availability	2 why = resource	1 who = provider
			Providers specializing in processing linen for healthcare
X +, X -	X +	X +	X +, Y +

The hospital expects to see a commercial laundry operation behind the promises of stacks of clean linen (enrichment) and the cleaning of soiled ones (enhancement). And not just any laundry, but one with the capabilities and resources able to handle large loads of healthcare linen. And will there be agents who are deployed across the hospital to facilitate the use of the service?

Figure 25
1 Who is making the promise?

The laundry expects to find a healthcare operation that justifies the fixed monthly payments and the fee per stack of clean linen. Then of course, given the number of beds, departments, physicians, and nurses, there will be large loads of soiled linen, and clean stacks that deplete daily. Knowing who the customers and users are, the laundry can develop a sense of what outcomes and experiences it will have to promise in return for the payments. Knowing who the provider and its agents are, the hospital has a sense of what it may have to promise, in terms of the volume of demand and payments. It also knows that it will have to permit the laundry staff, trucks, and carts, access to its facilities to make it easier for them to support its staff.

2 Why are they willing to?

Knowing who is making the promise clarifies why they are willing to make it, and why they may be able to keep it. Artifacts and events and the underlying needs are why customers promise demand. Capabilities and resources, or the abilities to fulfill customer needs, are why service providers are able to promise supply. Answers to the *question of why* establish the basis upon which the service exists.

Figure 26
Step 2

3 how

1 who   2 why

<why = artifact>	such as gowns, towels, and sheets for instance. <why>
<why = event>	Staff then immediately need to have clean linen for patients and for themselves. </why>
<why = capability>	a special process with a careful balance of chemicals, temperature, and pH levels. </why>
<why = resource>	industrial-scale equipment and large amounts of energy, water, chemicals, and detergents. </why>

In this case, the role the linen plays in healthcare is why the hospital is willing to arrange demand for performance and affordance. The number and type of linen, the way it gets soiled, and the policies and procedures that require the changing of linen, are why the hospital is able to promise the patterns necessary for the laundry to maintain the operational tempo on the front stage (the hospital) and the back stage (laundry facility). Similarly, the

1 who = customer	2 why = artifact	3 how = task	4 what = enhancement
Hospitals are therefore willing to pay for the processing of soiled linen and adequate supplies of clean linen	Such as gowns, towels, and sheets for instance		
X -, Y -	Y -	Y -	Y +, Y -
2 why = event	1 who = user	4 what = commission	3 how = activity
Staff then immediately need to have clean linen for patients and for themselves	Patients, physicians, nurses, and other staff, make daily use of linen		
X -	X -, Y -	Y +, Y -	Y +
3 how = access	4 what = provision	1 who = agent	2 why = capability
		Teams who take full responsibility for the soiled and clean linen	A special process with a careful balance of chemicals, temperature, and pH levels
X -	X +, X -	X +, Y +	Y +
4 what = enrichment	3 how = availability	2 why = resource	1 who = provider
		Industrial-scale equipment and large amounts of energy, water, chemicals, and detergents	Providers specializing in processing linen for healthcare
X +, X -	X +	X +	X +, Y +

laundry's commitment to advanced facilities and infrastructure, a highly-skilled workforce, and compliant processes, is why they are willing and able to promise the hospital a dependable supply of clean linen, and the staging and handling necessary to support the policies and procedures.

Figure 27
2 Why are they willing to?

Why someone is willing and able to make a promise depends on who they are. The two factors together define the motivations behind the promises, and the potential for demand or supply. Who determines why, and why determines how, and how determines what: how things will fall into arrangements and therefore what good will come from them. The factors of how and what define expectations. The motivations of each side (the potential) set the expectations (actual) for the other side. Bringing the diagonals of the 4x frame back into focus, the motivations are split, and the expectations are joined: the splitting of performance and affordance and the joining of demand and supply.

3 How will they keep the promise?

Why someone is making a promise leads to the question of how they will actually keep it. For service providers, the implications are: how needs will become actual instances of demand, and how the task is to be performed, what access will be given, and what it will actually look like. For customers, the implications are: how abilities will become actual instances of supply, how the activity performs the task, the availability that provides for access, and what it will actually look like. Implied in how are when and where. Activities, tasks, availability and access together actually form the performances and affordances, or how a service actually gets the job done.

Figure 28
Step 3

4 what   3 how

1 who   2 why

<how = access>   stacks of clean linen within easy reach of physicians and nurses. </how>

<how = task>   they need to be carefully cleaned and sterilized. </how>

<how = activity>   sorting, washing, drying, inspection, ironing, and folding. </how>

<how = availability>   machine cycles, work shifts, and trips to the hospital. </how>

The task of cleaning and sterilizing soiled linen, its types and quantities, when and where it piles up, and how soiled it will be, set expectations for performance. When and where stacks of clean linen get used up, how quickly they deplete, their types and quantities, and how clean they need to be, how many stacks and how high they should be, set expectations for affordance. On the sup-

1 who = customer Hospitals are therefore willing to pay for the processing of soiled linen and adequate supplies of clean linen X -, Y -	**2 why = artifact** Such as gowns, towels, and sheets for instance Y -	3 how = task They need to be carefully cleaned and sterilized Y -	**4 what = enhancement** Y +, Y -
2 why = event Staff then immediately need to have clean linen for patients and for themselves X -	**1 who = user** Patients, physicians, nurses, and other staff, make daily use of linen X -, Y -	**4 what = commission** Y +, Y -	3 how = activity Sorting, washing, drying, inspection, ironing, and folding Y +
3 how = access Stacks of fresh linen within their easy reach X -	**4 what = provision** X +, X -	**1 who = agent** Teams who take full responsibility for the soiled and clean linen X +, Y +	**2 why = capability** A special process with a careful balance of chemicals, temperature, and pH levels Y +
4 what = enrichment X +, X -	3 how = availability Machine cycles, work shifts, and trips to the hospital X +	**2 why = resource** Industrial-scale equipment and large amounts of energy, water, chemicals, and detergents X +	**1 who = provider** Providers specializing in processing linen for healthcare X +, Y +

ply side, the activities of removing, transporting, sorting, washing, drying, inspecting, ironing, and folding, set expectations for performance. Given the nature of the artifacts, when and where such activities will happen, and at what speed and scale, are important to the hospital, even if implied. As part of the promise, the laundry maintains controls to prevent cross-contamination

Figure 29
3 How will they keep the promise?

at any stage. The capacity cycles of all the activities, the labor shifts, and the round trips the carts and trucks make to the hospital, are how the provider promises the availability of its resources. Together they set expectations for how the affordances will happen, to stay ahead of how the stacks of clean linen get used up across the hospital.

Each side can visualize and verify how the other side will keep their promises from why they are able to make them. Being specialized in the healthcare business, the laundry can visualize the rhythmic filling up of the soiled closets, and the emptying of the clean closets and carts – because they also understand why demand can be that way. In the imagination of the provider is the time-lapse animation of demand. Similarly, the hospital can imagine how the laundry will meet their needs, knowing why it is possible to do so: the computer-controlled batch process, the staging areas that maintain separation between the clean and soiled linen, the careful inspection; and the systems the laundry has in place for the logistics of replenishment.

Embedded within the how, are the risks and costs for whoever will accept the promise, because of the dependencies and interactions. Therefore, how the promise is kept will influence whether what is being offered is attractive enough or not. If the how turns out to be too risky, then the what needs to compensate for that. Therefore, the how and the what of the promises define the risks and rewards, which in the case of services, translate into outcomes and experiences.

4 What can the other side expect?

The four promises are ultimately about what the other side can reasonably expect in terms of outcomes and experiences. What the promise is good for, or what good comes out of it, determines the chances of acceptance. Expectations are set at two levels. At one level, customers and service providers are negotiating the quality of outcomes, in terms of the cleanliness of the linen and the adequacy of the stacks. At another level, on behalf of their beneficiaries, employees and agents are also negotiating the quality of experiences: the ease and effort with which hospital and laundry staff can set up the performances and affordances.

To agree on the quality of outcomes and experiences, they must agree on the quality of payments or price.

1 who = customer Hospitals are therefore willing to pay for the processing of soiled linen and adequate supplies of clean linen X -, Y -	**2 why = artifact** Such as gowns, towels, and sheets for instance Y -	**3 how = task** They need to be carefully cleaned and sterilized Y -	**4 what = enhancement** Pay the laundry a management fee for converting soiled linen into clean linen Y +, Y -
2 why = event Staff then immediately need to have clean linen for patients and for themselves X -	**1 who = user** Patients, physicians, nurses, and other staff, make daily use of linen X -, Y -	**4 what = commission** Place soiled linen in bags and bins marked for the soiled closet, from where the laundry staff can pick up the linen Y +, Y -	**3 how = activity** Sorting, washing, drying, inspection, ironing, and folding Y +
3 how = access Stacks of fresh linen within their easy reach X -	**4 what = provision** Stack the linen in clean closets and exchange carts so hospital staff can quickly grab what they need X +, X -	**1 who = agent** Teams who take full responsibility for the soiled and clean linen X +, Y +	**2 why = capability** A special process with a careful balance of chemicals, temperature, and pH levels Y +
4 what = enrichment Pay a convenience fee per stack for an adequate stock of clean linen … X +, X -	**3 how = availability** Machine cycles, work shifts, and trips to the hospital X +	**2 why = resource** Industrial-scale equipment and large amounts of energy, water, chemicals, and detergents X +	**1 who = provider** Providers specializing in processing linen for healthcare X +, Y +

<what = commission> simply place soiled linen in bags and bins marked for the soiled closet. </what>

Figure 30
4 What can the other side expect?

<what = commission> pick up the linen from the soiled closet. </what>

Figure 31
Step 4

4 what   3 how

1 who   2 why

<what = provision>   stack the linen in clean closets and
                              exchange carts across the hospital.
                              </what>

<what = provision>   that way the hospital staff can quickly
                              grab what they need and be with pa-
                              tients. </what>

<what = enrichment>   an adequate stock of clean linen
                              across the hospital at all times. </what>

<what = enrichment>   the hospital offers to pay a conve-
                              nience fee per stack. </what>

<what = enhancement>   pay the laundry a management fee.
                              </what>

<what = enhancement>   convert soiled linen into clean linen.
                              </what>

In general, users and agents share the experiences. Therefore, they agree to make things as easy and effortless as possible for each other, under the principle of »help me help you to help me«. In this case, the procedures are already quite simple. For performance, hospital staff submit the linen by promptly placing it in bags and bins marked for the soiled closet. Laundry staff agree to promptly pick up the linen from there and arrange for the commission to be sent to the laundry facility, where the performances are to be staged. For affordance, the laundry staff fill the gaps in the stacks of clean linen with fresh stock from the laundry. They provision the gaps in such a way that hospital staff can quickly grab what they need and be with patients. Clean and soft fabric keeps appearing, as if the stacks were magical.

The hospital and the laundry together gain from patients and hospital staff having the clean linen they need, as and when they need it. The payoff for the hospital is in terms of safety and comfort across its care settings. The gains materialize in two ways: enhancement and enrichment. The enhancement is in soiled linen returning in a clean and sterilized state. It is also in the reduced risks of infections, diseases and discomfort. The enrichment is in the stacks of clean linen. On both accounts, the hospital is better off. The benefits flow in both directions. The laundry receives regular payments for enhancement and for enrichment. The payments may be against a single invoice but are separately considered. It is worth noting again why performances and affordances are separate from the same. The soiling of the linen leads to shortcomings and shortfalls – the soiled linen become artifacts, and the gap they then create in a stack of clean linen, trigger the events.

There is a feedback loop between *who* (1) and *what* (4). Over a number of instances or over a period of time, each side evaluates the gains and pains they accumulate. Based on such evaluations, they may value that particular set of promises a bit more, or a bit less.[42] When customers and service providers are evaluating each other's promises for the first time, the attractiveness of what is being promised depends on who is looking at it. So, for example, every hospital values the outcomes and experiences the laundry promises. They all care about their linen in the same way. However, depending on the scale and scope of their operations, and other particular constraints, the hospitals may differ in what they are willing to promise in return, including what they're willing to pay. The laundry in turn may similarly attach different values to what different hospitals offer, because of the associated costs and risks. Perhaps they have optimized their entire system to better serve large hospitals over the small ones. These are important considerations.

The four factors – framed as simple questions – make it possible to extract information from narratives. The quality of the extracts depends on how good the narratives are – how well-written, informative, and complete. In practice, we would rely on multiple sources of information, including but not limited to, stories, transcripts, field notes, memos, reports, plans, and policy statements. The information is then 'processed' by applying design thinking to question, reason, and surmise. We then have concise statements that define a service concept. We didn't do all that in the preceding example. We simply 'cut and paste' the highlighted statements, focusing more on the manner in which the detail fills the frame, simultaneously across the four promises.

Closing the loop

Figure 32
Closed loop

4 what		3 how
1 who		2 why

HOW

WHO   WHY   WHO   WHY

WHAT HOW   WHAT HOW

WHO   WHY   WHO   WHY

WHAT HOW

WHO WHY

6

Elements

6

The 16x frame is for developing and improving the design of a service through broad and inclusive participation across groups, functions, and disciplines.

It is useful for teams across the layers of an enterprise to develop a shared understanding of the concept of a service. They do so by forming 16 definitive statements, covering the four promises and their four factors. The statements represent the 16 elements of design found in every service. Everything that could be said to be a service can be summarized under them. This way, the 16x can be useful for teams to first develop a single shared coherent concept. Each layer can then interpret the statements and elaborate them by adding detail. Then, no matter how different the details look from one layer to another, they all have a common conceptual basis – they implement the same four promises expressed through the same 16 statements.

16x is an 'open structure' that facilitates collaboration across groups – diverse and dispersed – without strict rules on how collaboration should take place. The language and format provide a neutral ground for the collaboration; a particular discipline cannot dominate. While it may be much harder for such teams to 'work together' (due to differences in tools, terminology, models, metrics, and metaphors) studies have shown that they actually perform better. When a team is diverse enough, everybody is an outsider. *More imaginations are in play.* There would be new realizations that would be unlikely to occur in homogenous groups operating with a common set of axioms, rules, and assumptions. More kinds of issues surface, concerning rules, regulations, ethics, cultures, environments, economics, finance, politics, and physics.[43]

The 16x frame

Format

Every panel of the 16x frame should have a valid entry. An entry is valid when it is corroborated by two other statements. *Completing a 16x frame is therefore like solving a puzzle.* You can start anywhere on the frame – with elements you are most certain about – and then progressively fill up the frame, using critical reasoning to defining adjoining statements. *If this, then that.* Information available to us is often ambiguous, unclear, or incomplete. The gaps and conflicts that emerge prompt further discussion. More thought, more inquiry, or further research. The more time we take in defining and understanding the problem, using our own frame of reference in developing conceptual structure, the more likely we are to achieve a creative result (Dorst & Cross, 2001). It is important to take time to fill up the frame. The statements may require revisions – several times even – until each one of them makes sense by itself and when combined with two other statements. A completed 16x frame is therefore indicative of a certain level of effort – evidence of the amount of thinking that has gone into the concept – analogous to 'proof of work' in cryptography.

Language

There isn't a universal language for describing services, or a periodic table of elements. Different functions and disciplines have their own terminology and ways of describing the various elements of a service. *To fully leverage the richness and diversity of teams, it is important to have a neutral terminology.* Therefore, the following 16 words form the vocabulary of the 16x: customer, user, artifact, event, provider, agent, capability, resource, activity, task, availability, event, enhancement, enrichment, commission, and provision.

Code

In addition to a label, each element also has an alphanumeric code based on four numbers and eight letters. The code has several purposes, the simplest of which is giving us a shorter way to refer to the elements. The code also stores the standard definition of a 16x element and ascribes it to the label next to it. This means that even if other words are used as labels, within the context of 16x they still have the same meaning as the original words. For example, in some domains, customers are referred to as »clients« or »payers«, and providers as »agencies« or »carriers«. Such labels, when placed next to 1M and 1V, then assume the standard meanings of customer and provider, based on the stan-

1M customer	2A artifact	3AC task	4MV enhancement
Those who pay for the service and benefit from the outcomes	Things with shortcomings, or why there will be demand for performances	How the artifact needs to be acted upon; actual instances of demand	What the outcome of a performance is; product of activity and task
X -, Y -	Y -	Y -	Y +, Y -
2T event	**1U user**	**4UG commission**	**3CA activity**
Things with shortfalls, or why there will be demand for affordances	Those who have the privilege to make use of the service	What users and agents go through (experience) to set up activity and task	How the capability performs the task; actual instances of supply
X -	X -, Y -	Y +, Y -	Y +
3TR access	**4GU provision**	**1G agent**	**2C capability**
How the event needs to have access to the resource; actual instances of demand	What users and agents go through (experience) to set up availability and access	Those who facilitate and control the use of the service	Things with skills, or why there will be supply for performances
X -	X +, X -	X +, Y +	Y +
4VM enrichment	**3RT availability**	**2R resource**	**1V provider**
What the outcome of an affordance is; product of availability and access	How the resource is made available for access; actual instances of supply	Things with surpluses, or why there will be supply for affordances	Things with surpluses, or why there will be supply for affordances
X +, X -	X +	X +	X +, Y +

dard definitions. The code also indicates how elements relate to each other. The inputs to an element are the two other elements that influence it or cause a change. For example, the activity (3CA) and the task (3AC) influence the experience of users and agents with respect to the performance (4UG). All 16 elements have two inputs each. The inputs in series form the sequences.

Figure 33
The 16x frame

The dual of an element in one aspect – performance or affor-dance – is an element that relates to it in the other aspect. For example, tasks (3AC) and access' (3TR) are duals of each oth-er, as are capabilities (2C) and resources (2R). From one, we can understand the other. When we understand one, we better un-derstand the other. The counterpart of an element on one side (demand or supply) is an element that is related to it on the other side. For example, users (1U) and agents (1G) are counterparts, as are customers (1M) and providers (1V). This way of understand-ing elements of demand means that we can better understand the elements of supply, and vice versa.

Numbers
1, 2, 3, 4
Correspond to the four factors: who, why, how and what

Letters
M, U, G, V, C, R, A, T
Correspond to people and things: customer, user, agent, provider, capability, resource, artifact and event

Codes

1M	2A	3AC	4MV
2T	1U4	4UG	3CA
3TR	4GU	1G	2C
4VM	3RT	2R	1V

Correspond to the 16 words that form the vocabulary of the 16x frame.

The leitmotiv

The numbers in the code correspond to the four factors of a promise: (1) who, (2) why, (3) how and (4) what. They group the 16 elements according to the factors and relate them to each other across the frame. For example, 2T, 2A, 2C and 2R are references to the four types of »things« in a service or the reason why there is potential for it. Most importantly, the numbers define a *leitmo-tiv* across the frame: *1-2-3-4*.

This recurring pattern binds together the 16 statements cohe-sively into a single concept. It encodes the inherent dynamics in every service, that drive its behaviors across space and time; the way instances of demand and supply come together to form performances and affordances, and the way outcomes and ex-

1 M	2 A	3 AC	**4 MV**
2 T	1 U	**4 UG**	3 CA
3 TR	**4 GU**	1 G	2 C
4 VM	3 RT	2 R	1 V

Customer	Artifact	Task	**Enhancement**
Event	User	**Commis-sion**	Activity
Access	**Provision**	Agent	Capability
Enrichment	Availability	Resource	Provider

Figure 34
Labels and codes

periences materialize. It defines the cyclical rhythm or heartbeat of a service. It also defines feedback loops. Without the *leitmotiv*, the 16x frame is just another grid.

There are eight such sequences within 16x, each forming a short narrative in the who-why-how-what format (or the scope of a promise). In pairs, the narratives cover the four promises (X +, Y +, X -, Y -) . Those can then be joined (in groups of four) to form longer narratives about outcomes, experiences, performances, affordances, demand, and supply. All eight of them together can then form a »story« about the service as a whole. That way, the 1-2-3-4 sequence also indicates the different ways to read across the frame (with a finger trace), which isn't simply 'left to right' as in the case of most Western languages.

Services are agreements between people and arrangements between things. The middle part of each sequence (2-3) represents »things in arrangement«, and the two ends of each sequence (1-, -4) correspond to »people in agreement«. Agreements bracket or hold the arrangements.

	Demand for (-)	Supply for (+)
Performance (Y)	1M - 2A - 3AC - 4MV 1U - 2A - 3AC - 4UG	1V - 2C - 3CA - 4MV 1G - 2C - 3CA - 4UG
Affordance (X)	1U - 2T - 3TR - 4GU 1M - 2T - 3TR - 4VM	1G - 2R - 3RT - 4GU 1V - 2R - 3RT - 4VM

With elements in common, the eight sequences are interlocked, giving the 16x frame its puzzle-like quality. The cross references bring out inconsistencies, conflicts, and contradictions, forcing teams to slow down and give it further thought. Just as in puzzles, they can also speed up things. There may be clues, clarifications, and corroborations. That way, using what they know about the elements they are quite certain about, teams can then make inductive and abductive leaps to fill in

SERVICES ARE AGREEMENTS

BETWEEN PEOPLE

AND ARRANGEMENTS

BETWEEN THINGS.

Figure 35 (left)
Sequences

Figure 36 (right)
Feedback loops

the blanks. Having gone through the pains of solving the puzzle, a completed 16x frame signifies a certain level of confidence in the design concept. The »proof of work«.

Figure 35 (left)
Sequences

Figure 36 (right)
Feedback loops

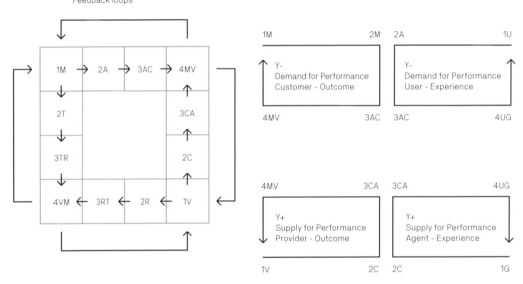

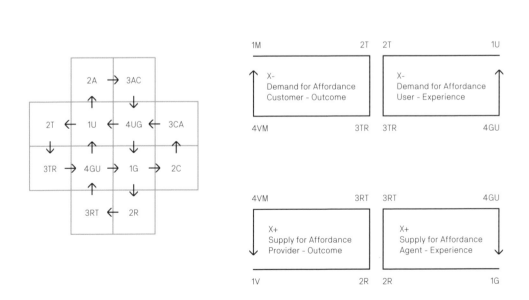

Parts catalog

16 parts make a service whole. This catalog defines the parts. It is also a glossary for the 16x frame. The definitions are abstract by nature to allow room for interpretation, given the great variety in services, including many that are very technical in nature, involving machines as users and agents. In that sense, the definitions are clues on what to look for when identifying the 16 elements in documents and discussions. Some of the words describing the elements repeatedly appear across the definitions, to highlight the similarities and differences, especially with respect to the duals and counterparts across the frame. The nuances within these definitions appear over time across several interpretations.

Customer

1M

Those who pay for the service and benefit from the outcomes. Customers pay for the service because they are the ones who ultimately benefit from the outcomes. They may be owners of the artifact or event, or simply feel responsible for improving its condition or state. They procure privileges for using the service, which they may themselves use (»the customer is the user«) or give them to others (»customer is not the user«). As groups or as individuals, customers are the entities behind the agreement, responsible for evaluating the quality of outcomes and making timely payments. They decide whether to continue the use of the service or terminate the agreement.

Promises	X-, Y-
Groups	motivation, agreement, outcome, performance, affordance, demand
Inputs	4MV Enhancement, 4VM Enrichment
Dual	1U User
Counterpart	1V Provider

User

1U

Those who have the privilege to make use of the service. Users are the ones who actually invoke the service and redeem the procured privileges. To do so, they engage agents in dialog and interaction, through touchpoints, channels, and interfaces. As part of the agreement, users are expected to make the necessary effort and bring to bear artifacts and events, for the performances and affordances, through the dual acts of commission and provision. The dialog and interaction influence their user experience. Their personas, priorities, and preferences influence the levels of ease and effort for service agents. They are expected to empathize with the agents with whom they share the experiences. Users can be groups or individuals, and humans or machines.

Promises   X-, Y-
Groups   motivation, agreement, experience, performance, affordance, demand
Inputs   4UG Commission, 4GU Provision
Dual   1M Customer
Counterpart   1G Agent

Provider

1V

Those who offer the service and get paid for the outcomes. Providers are confident about performances and affordances because of the capabilities and resources they control. They employ agents to facilitate and control the use of the service. They are the ones who grant user privileges, which agents subsequently recognize and redeem as part of the agreement. As groups or individuals, providers are the entities behind the agreement, assuring the outcomes and accepting the payments. The quality of the outcomes for providers is seen in terms of the payments they receive for the service, whether in cash or in kind. They evaluate the quality of outcomes and determine whether they should continue to provide the service or have grounds to terminate the agreement.

Promises   X+, Y+
Groups   motivation, agreement, outcome, performance, affordance, supply
Inputs   4MV Enhancement, 4VM Enrichment
Dual   1G Agent
Counterpart   1V Customer

Agent

1G

Those who facilitate and control the use of the service. Agents act on behalf of the provider. They engage users in dialog and interaction through touchpoints, channels, and interfaces. They recognize users, respond to their requests, and redeem their procured privileges. Based on user input, they coordinate and control performances and affordances, working in concert with others involved in the background. They are expected to empathize with users with whom they share experiences. Agents can be groups or individuals, and humans or machines; whomever the provider can effectively delegate responsibility and authority to, in order to facilitate and control the use of the service.

Promises	X+, Y+
Groups	motivation, agreement, experience, performance, affordance, supply
Inputs	4UG Commission, 4GU Provision
Dual	1V Provider
Counterpart	1U User

Things with shortcomings, or why there will be demand for performances. Artifacts create the actual instances of demand for performance, when they need to be rendered to a preferred state. They are the reason why customers pay for performances. Artifacts define the task to be performed. Tangible or intangible, fixed or moving, artifacts are on the demand side of performances. In some services, it is the physical or mental states of people that receive enhancement; they are the things people value within themselves, such as feelings, emotions, physical presence, and good health. In some services, artifacts and events are often one and the same thing, projecting both types of needs.

Artifact

2A

Promises	Y-
Groups	motivation, arrangement, outcome, experience, performance, demand
Inputs	1M Customer, 1U User
Dual	2T Event
Counterpart	2C Capability

Things with shortfalls, or why there will be demand for affordances. Events are the reason why customers pay for affordance. They create demand in the form of the need to have access to a resource at a particular time and place. Tangible or intangible, fixed or moving, events are on the demand side of affordances. In some services, it is the physical or mental states of people that receive enrichment; they are the things people value within themselves, such as knowledge and status, and feelings such as safety, privacy, and comfort. They may also value food, medicine, and entertainment. In some services, artifacts and events are often one and the same thing, projecting both types of needs (such as a patient receiving a timely vaccine through injection).

Event

2T

Promises	X-
Groups	motivation, arrangement, outcome, experience, affordance, demand
Inputs	1M Customer, 1U User
Dual	2A Artifact
Counterpart	2R Resource

Resource

2R

Things with surpluses, or why there will be supply for affordances. Resources are why providers are confident about promising affordances. The availability of a resource at a particular time and place is its primary virtue. Therefore, staging and holding adequate surpluses is a fundamental part of the design. Tangible or intangible, fixed or moving, resources are the supply side of affordances. How they are made available depends on the degree of affordance. The mere presence of a resource can make available intangibles such as safety, comfort, authority, and trust. Other resources are environments within which events take place. Resources often give capabilities their capacities, physical forms, and presence.

Promises	X+
Groups	motivation, arrangement, outcome, experience, affordance, supply
Inputs	1V Provider, 1G Agent
Dual	2C Capability
Counterpart	2T Event

Capability

2C

Things with skills, or why there will be supply for performances. Capabilities are why providers are confident about promising performances. They store the potential for activities that perform the task of rendering an artifact to a preferred state. By itself, a capability is an intangible thing; it represents the ability to accurately reproduce a desired effect, time and again. In reality, capabilities are embedded in other things (or people) in the form of skills or competence. To produce actual instances of activities, capabilities may require physical forms and presences of a certain kind (for example, physicians and robots skillfully performing surgery). Tangible or intangible, fixed or moving, capabilities form the supply side of performance. Capabilities empower resources. The two types of assets are often one and the same.[44]

Promises	Y-
Groups	motivation, arrangement, outcome, experience, performance, supply
Inputs	1V Provider, 1G Agent
Dual	2R Resource
Counterpart	2C Artifact

Things with shortcomings, or why there will be demand for per-formances. Tasks are calls for action, and how artifacts become available to be handled and acted upon. Completion of the task results in the enhancement of the artifact. In some cases, the activity comes to the task. In other cases, the task needs to be where the activity is performed. Bringing them together is part of the arrangement. Tasks represent varying levels of difficulty and risk in terms of when and where and how quickly they need to be performed, or how carefully the artifacts are to be handled. They could be hazardous, or sensitive to damage. Or they could involve the physical and mental states of people. A task can trigger the need for access, or the two can be one and the same. Tasks de-fine demand patterns for performance, including what the cus-tomer is willing to pay for that aspect of the service.

Task

3AC

Promises	Y-
Groups	expectation, arrangement, outcome, experience, performance, demand
Inputs	2A Artifact (in two separate sequences)
Dual	3TR Access
Counterpart	3CA Activity

How the capability performs the task; actual instances of sup-ply. Activities are the means by which capabilities perform the task to enhance the value of the artifact. They are actual instanc-es of supply. The activity commences when agents have custody and control of the artifact. When and where the activity is per-formed sometimes depend on the nature of the task. Part of the arrangement is the proper staging and handling of the task for the rendering process. The performance of some activities may require the artifact to be temporary unavailable for use. Some activities may first require the availability of a resource, as with-out it the performance is not possible. Completion of the activity should produce within the artifact the desired effect. Activities

Activity

3CA

define supply patterns for performance, including what the provider is willing to accept for that aspect of the service.

Promises	Y+
Groups	expectation, arrangement, outcome, experience, performance, supply
Inputs	2C Capability (in two separate sequences)
Dual	3RT Availability
Counterpart	3AC Task

Access

3TR

How the event needs to have access to the resource; actual instances of demand. Access is how an event expresses its need to have access to a resource at a particular place and time. It also defines the degree of affordance, or the extent to which customers have flexibility and control over the use of the resource, as a temporary asset. At the highest degree, customers acquire the resource without having to exit, vacate, release, or return. In some cases, the resource is supplied or staged within the event (as a utility or good), while in other cases the event is staged within the resource (acting as an environment). Allowing access may pose a risk in the case of resources that are hazardous or sensitive to damage. The affordance could involve the physical and mental presence of people. Access may first require a task to be performed, or the two can be one and the same. Access defines demand patterns for affordance, including what the customer is willing to pay for that aspect of the service.

Promises	X-
Groups	expectation, arrangement, outcome, experience, affordance, demand
Inputs	2T Event (in two separate sequences)
Dual	3AC Task
Counterpart	3RT Availability

Availability

3RT

How the resource is made available for access; actual instances of supply. Availability is how a resource is actually made available to an event for a period of time, at the end of which the access terminates. In some cases, the affordance permanently transfers the ownership of the resource to customers who acquire it as an asset. Availability can be mostly about time, or largely about location or place. One or the other dimension may dominate. In any case, availability requires the maintenance of adequate levels of surplus, a portion of which the affordance allocates and activates to the event. In some cases, the availability represents a window of opportunity within which the access is possible, or the event can occur. In other cases, the event defines the window of opportunity. Availability may first require an activity to be performed, or the two can be one and the same. Availabilities define supply patterns for affordance, including what the provider is willing to accept for that aspect of the service.

Promises	X+
Groups	expectation, arrangement, outcome, experience, affordance, supply
Inputs	2R Resource (in two separate sequences)
Dual	3CA Activity
Counterpart	3TR Access

Commission

What users and agents go through (experience) to set up activities and tasks. Commission is the process users and agents go through to set up activities and tasks for performances. Users give agents custody and control of the artifact. The nature of the performance determines the steps users and agents have to go through, along with when and where. Assigning a task by itself may implicitly authorize agents to activate the capability and initiate performance. Or, the agents may require a more explicit signature. That determines whether they can engage remotely or have to meet in-person, and if their dialog and interaction can be asynchronous or tightly coupled. In many services, the commission is automatic or implied when the artifact appears within the stage where the activity is being performed. Upon fulfillment, agents may have to release the artifact and facilitate its return.

4UG

Promises	Y+, Y-
Groups	expectation, agreement, experience, performance, demand, supply
Inputs	3AC Task, 3CA Capability
Dual	4GU Provision
Counterpart	Not applicable

Provision

4GU

What users and agents go through (experience) to set up avail-ability and access. Provisioning is the process users and agents go through to set up availability and access for affordance. Agents give users custody and control of the resource, by allocating capacity and activating privilege. Users are then able to exploit the resource within the event. The nature of the affordance determines the steps users and agents have to go through, along with when and where. Unblocking access to the resource, or not actively preventing users from reaching it, may implicitly authorize its use. How much control users need to have, and how much agents retain, determine whether they can engage remotely, or have to meet in-person, and if their dialog and interaction can be asynchronous or tightly coupled. Upon fulfillment, agents may have to take back control of the resource or facilitate its return.

Promises	X+, X-
Groups	expectation, agreement, experience, affordance, demand, supply
Inputs	3TR Access, 3RT Availability
Dual	4UG Commission
Counterpart	Not applicable

Enhancement

4MV

What the outcome of a performance is; product of activity and task. Customers verify the outcome by finding their artifact to be in the preferred condition or state. The results of enhancement may be tangible, intangible, visible or invisible, within the artifact. Regardless, the fixing of the shortcoming should be easily perceived by the customer, or readily felt from the underlying asset being more useful and valuable. Evidence of the activity having been performed, by itself, may not be sufficient. The gains (or avoided losses) that materialize from the outcome are the immediate or eventual payoff for the customer. They justify the payment for performance.

Promises	Y+, Y-
Groups	expectation, agreement, outcome, performance, demand, supply
Inputs	3AC Task, 3CA Activity
Dual	4VM Enrichment
Counterpart	Not applicable

What the outcome of an affordance is; product of availability and access. Customers verify the outcome by finding their event to be in a »richer« state. The results of enrichment may be tangible, intangible, visible or invisible, within the event. Regardless, the filling of the shortfall should be easily perceived by the customer, or readily felt from the underlying asset being more useful and valuable. Evidence of the availability of the resource, by itself, may not be sufficient. The gains (or avoided losses) that materialize from the outcome are the immediate or eventual payoff for the customer. They justify the payment for affordance.

Promises	X+, X-
Groups	expectation, agreement, outcome, affordance, demand, supply
Inputs	3TR Access, 3RT Availability
Dual	4MV Enhancement
Counterpart	Not applicable

In some cases, enhancement follows enrichment, or vice versa. In other cases, they happen at once. They are the outcomes the two sides share but independently evaluate from their own perspectives. The quality of outcomes influences how customers and service providers feel about their agreements. That is why 4MV and 4VM are inputs to 1M and 1V. Similarly, in some cases, provisioning follows commission, or vice versa. In other cases, they happen at once. Together they amount to the experiences the two sides share, but independently evaluate. The quality of experiences influences how users and agents feel about similar promises in the future. That is why 4UG and 4GU are inputs to 1U and 1G. Enhancement, enrichment, commission and provision, together define a set of outcomes and experiences and therefore the essential parts of a service agreement.

Enrichment

4VM

Diagonal elements

7

Frames

7

Stories are a good way to communicate ideas and concepts, across the usual barriers between functions, disciplines, and cultures. It is a reason why they are an important part of product design and development.

Stories and frames go hand in hand. Stories generate frames. Frames generate stories. Together they show how problem and solution co-exist, and complete each other, within the concept of a service.

We may start with stories of the future, describing how the problem and solution might evolve over time, based on scenarios and trends. We then use the stories to create a set of *future frames*. A similar exercise generates stories and frames describing problems and solutions as they are today. By comparing the frames of today with those of tomorrow, we then develop a clear idea of what must change and in what way, in terms of the 16 elements of design. Such exercises can be very useful toward the development of product road maps, policies, and strategies.

Two groups working separately can write stories about a service – one group writing from the customer and user perspectives, and the other from those of the provider and the agent. The groups then use their stories to fill out 16x frames. They then get together and compare them, focusing on the similarities and differences. The discussions that follow lead to the development of a *consensus frame*, reinforcing the similarities and reconciling the differences. The stories from the new frame thus codify the consensus.

We have seen how a story can generate a 16x frame (with the hospital linen case). Now let's see the reverse happening – a 16x frame generating a story. We start by looking at one of the most commonly found services – a retail store offering an assortment of goods – with child-like imagination, just so we understand what makes it a service.

Time to Ottolenghi

11:35

Khairun opens her favorite Ottolenghi book to a recipe she has never tried. It calls for quinoa. Khairun reaches into her kitchen shelf and there it is, waiting to be cooked. The recipe also requires some sheep's milk feta cheese. Khairun reaches into her fridge. Where is it? Not where it's supposed to be. She rolls up her sleeves and extends her hand, so it goes all the way to the back of the fridge, through it, into the kitchen wall, out of her home, across the neighborhood (a quick wave to a neighbor), travels two blocks, and opens the door of a back-up fridge inside the local grocery store. And there it is! Khairun grabs a small packet of the ingredient and retracts her hands to retrieve the feta to the kitchen counter where she is preparing the dish. As her hand leaves the store, it makes two simple gestures: it gives the store money and data. The money rewards the effort that goes into keeping things, so they are »up for grabs«. The data adds to the intelligence that stocks the shelves.

It's not just Khairun's habits. Others in the vicinity do the same, whenever they reach for something and it's not there, in the fridge or on the shelf. As the retail end of supply chains, the store offers continuity in lifestyles and diets by locally 'caching' food in anticipation of needs. Everybody has access to the food for a fee. The fee has two components. The 'consider it your own' component is for the option of reaching into a store shelf and taking what you need, *as if it were your own*. Just like you do from a shelf at home. The 'make it your own' component is for you to carry on that pretense and carry the goods out of the store. Cache and carry. The shoppers are a loosely formed buyers' collective. There is no minimum purchase and yet everybody bears the cost of stocking the facility, so most of the time it has what they reach for. Their habits aggregated result in bulk purchases on part of the store. Local cultures, cuisines, seasons, and trends predict what the hand might be grabbing next. Every purchase adds a data point. As a result, the probability of Khairun and others not finding what they need when they need it, falls below a threshold.

1M customer	2A artifact	3AC task	4MV enhancement
Khairun enjoys a lifestyle and diet that keep her healthy, happy, and well within budget.	Some recipes call for ingredients that make her *mise en place* set up incomplete.	Buying the ingredients and bringing them home is necessary to make the meal.	When the items appear on a store receipt, the set up at home is soon complete; life goes uninterrupted.
X -, Y -	Y -	Y -	Y +, Y -
2T event	**1U user**	**4UG commission**	**3CA activity**
Not everything is at hand because she makes meals with fresh ingredients from a local store.	Often, the Ottolenghi fan picks a recipe she likes and then gathers things to prepare the meal.	Claiming those items at a store counter allows the cashier to process them for sale.	Scanning an item transfers the ownership of the good to the bill the buyer is going to pay.
X -	X -, Y -	Y +, Y -	Y +
3TR access	**4GU provision**	**1G agent**	**2C capability**
Buying only what a recipe needs to have, when needed, is often better for the Planet, purse, and plate.	The store layout, signage, and displays make it easy to find what you are looking for and claim it for yourself.	Store staff are there to ease the flow of goods through shelves and checkout counters.	The store's checkout system converts recipes and shopping lists into bags of groceries.
X -	X +, X -	X +, Y +	Y +
4VM enrichment	**3RT availability**	**2R resource**	**1V provider**
What is not in the kitchen is in the cart, within minutes of deciding what to make.	The goods are available in a variety of sizes, packages, and grades; priced and labeled for retail purchase	A fresh assortment of food is within easy reach of those who live close by; private stocks on public shelves.	As the retail end of supply chains, the store offers continuity in lifestyles and diets.
X +, X -	X +	X +	X +, Y +

Khairun and others could stock a lot more at home so their hands don't get tired from all that stretching. However, there is only so much shelf space at home and after a point the carrying costs of that inventory would be too high. There is another advantage. Many of the goods are perishable and have expiry dates. (Letting neighbors have access to your shelves might prevent food

Figure 37
11:35 Time to Ottolenghi

waste.) Goods are less likely to expire on a public shelf because someone or the other runs out of them. Fresher goods are in stock that way. There will still be some spoilage, but that cost is spread across the entire population. Over time the »elves behind the shelves« get good at making predictions, from all the data on past purchases. Google analyzes emails, searches, and text messages, to display personalized ads. The store analyzes past purchases to »display goods«. By understanding lifestyles and diets, the store maintains the right assortment of goods within easy reach; for the locals, their own *private public shelves* to grab from.

Story generation

There are eight 1-2-3-4 sequences through the frame. Each sequence generates a narrative or thread. Weaving the threads creates a story. The best order in which to combine them depends on the story and the storyteller. There is no other rule or restriction other than all eight threads should be included. A team with storytelling skills can create a most compelling one that communicates the concept of a service, based on their intimate knowledge of problem spaces and solution sets. The 16x frame affords them that opportunity.[45] Let's go through the exercise of pulling the eight threads from the 16x frame, and then weaving them together into a single story. This exercise has an additional purpose: practice with thinking in code and sequence.

This 16x frame of Khairun going grocery shopping is based on the following promises:

If you promise [(to cook) meals that need to have fresh ingredients] and [shopping lists that need to be bags of groceries], we promise [an assortment of fresh goods on shelves nearby] and [a convenient retail purchase].

We start with the thread 1M-2A-3AC-4MV ... in which the customer cares about performance.

1M   Khairun enjoys a lifestyle and diet that keep her healthy, happy, and well within budget.

2A   Some recipes call for ingredients that make her *mise en place* set up incomplete.

3AC   Buying the ingredients and bringing them home is neces-
       sary to make the meal.

4MV   When the items appear on a store receipt, the kitchen at
       home is soon replete; life goes uninterrupted.

Dropping the code references and joining the statements gives
us the narrative:

»Khairun enjoys a lifestyle and diet that keep her healthy, happy, and well within budget. Some recipes call for ingredients that
make her *mise en place* set up incomplete. Buying the ingredients and bringing them home is necessary to make the meal.
When the items appear on a store receipt, the kitchen at home is
soon replete; life goes uninterrupted.«

Next is the thread: 1M-2T-3TR-4VM ... in which the customer cares
about affordance.

1M   Khairun enjoys a lifestyle and diet that keep her healthy,
       happy, and well within budget.

2T   Not everything is at hand because she makes meals with
       fresh ingredients from a local store.

3TR   Buying only what a recipe needs to have, when needed, is
       often better for the Planet, purse, and plate.

4VM   What is not in the kitchen is in the cart, within minutes of
       deciding what to make.

Incorporating 1M-2T-3TR-4VM further develops the story:

»Khairun enjoys a lifestyle and diet that keep her healthy, happy, and well within budget. Some recipes call for ingredients that
make her *mise en place* set up incomplete. Not everything is at
hand because she makes meals with fresh ingredients from a local store. Buying only what a recipe needs to have, when needed, is often better for the Planet, purse, and plate. What is not
in the kitchen is in the cart, within minutes of deciding what to
make. Buying the ingredients and bringing them home is necessary to make the meal. When the items appear on a store receipt,
the kitchen at home is soon replete; life goes uninterrupted.« [46]

Next is the narrative or sequence 1U-2T-3TR-4GU ... in which the user cares about affordance.

1U   Often, the Ottolenghi fan picks a recipe she likes and then gathers things to prepare the meal.

2T   Not everything is at hand because she makes meals with fresh ingredients from a local store.

3TR   Buying only what a recipe needs to have, when needed, is often better for the Planet, purse, and plate.

4GU   The store layout, signage, and displays make it easy to find what you are looking for and claim it for yourself.

Incorporating the 1U-2T-3TR-4GU narrative gives us:

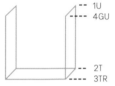
-- 1U
---- 4GU

-- 2T
---- 3TR

»Khairun enjoys a lifestyle and diet that keep her healthy, happy, and well within budget. Often, the Ottolenghi fan picks a recipe she likes and then gathers things to prepare the meal. Some recipes call for ingredients that make her *mise en place* set up incomplete. Not everything is at hand because she makes meals with fresh ingredients from a local store. Buying only what a recipe needs to have, when needed, is often better for the Planet, purse, and plate. The store layout, signage, and displays make it easy to find what you are looking for and claim it for yourself. What is not in the kitchen is in the cart, within minutes of deciding what to make. Buying the ingredients and bringing them home is necessary to make the meal. When the items appear on a store receipt, the kitchen at home is soon replete; life goes uninterrupted.«

Note in the last step, the statements 2T and 3TR are repeated – they are exactly the same from both the customer and user perspectives. That's because, in consumer services the customer and the user are often one and the same person.

Next is 1U-2A-3AC-4UG ... in which the user cares about performance.

As in the previous step, the statements 2A and 3AC are repeated. The only new statement to add is 4UG. This last statement explains how the ingredients that were in the cart end up both in a bag and on a receipt. It also completes the demand side of the story.

»Khairun enjoys a lifestyle and diet that keep her healthy, happy, and well within budget. Often, the Ottolenghi fan picks a recipe she likes and then gathers things to prepare the meal. Some recipes call for ingredients that make her *mise en place* set up incomplete. Not everything is at hand because she makes meals with fresh ingredients from a local store. Buying only what a recipe needs to have, when needed, is often better for the Planet, purse, and plate. The store layout, signage, and displays make it easy to find what you are looking for and claim it for yourself. What is not in the kitchen is in the cart, within minutes of deciding what to make. Buying the ingredients and bringing them home is necessary to make the meal. Claiming those items at a store counter allows the cashier to process them for sale. When the items appear on a store receipt, the kitchen at home is soon replete; life goes uninterrupted.«

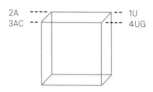

There are of course two sides to a story. The remaining four narratives tell the supply side of it. They are from the perspectives of the store (the provider) and its staff (the agents), about performance and affordance, concerning the outcomes and experiences. Let's keep a keen eye on how the two sides of the story join together with the four common statements: 4MV, 4VM, 4UG, and 4GU. Or, how demand meets supply with these four statements, which form the service agreement. Which is why they also correspond to the definitions of the outcomes and experiences. Here we are analyzing a completed 16x frame. In practice, the two sides of the story may be separately written or told, for example, by customers and service providers during a procurement process. Joining the two halves to make it one is then part of a collaborative approach to developing solutions that both sides will equally benefit from.

In this case, the supply side of the story begins with the local store, a retail operation, that assumes the risk of carrying an inventory of perishable goods so customers like Khairun can pursue the lifestyles and diets that make them happy. Like any retail business, location is of paramount importance, so the customer's hand doesn't have to stretch too far. It's about putting goods on a public shelf, keeping the doors open during hours that are convenient, and letting customers grab what they need. Availability is the name of the game. If a thing isn't available on a shelf when a customer's hand reaches out to grab it, then it doesn't matter how much of it exists elsewhere. Therefore, the number one job in retail is having the right assortment of goods available across shelves at any given moment (Brandes & Brandes, 2011). It is what makes Khairun's hand reach through a particular set of doors over others.

Since we now have the hang of it, let's take a brief look at the four narratives, and then incorporate them all at once into the story, and note how the customer's side of the story gets even better with the provider's side added.

1V-2R-3RT-4VM ... in which the provider cares about affordance.

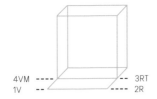

1V   As the retail end of supply chains, the store offers continuity in lifestyles and diets.

2R   A fresh assortment of food is within easy reach of those who live close by; private stocks on public shelves.

3RT The goods are available in a variety of sizes, packages, and grades; priced and labeled for retail sale.

4VM What is not in the kitchen is in the cart, within minutes of deciding what to make.

1V-2C-3CA-4MV ... in which the provider cares about performance.

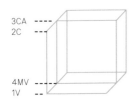

1V   As the retail end of supply chains, the store offers continuity in lifestyles and diets.

2C   The store's checkout system converts recipes and shopping lists into bags of groceries.

3CA Scanning an item transfers the ownership of the good to the bill the buyer is going to pay.

4MV When the items appear on a store receipt, the kitchen at home is soon replete; life goes uninterrupted.

1G-2R-3RT-4GU ... in which the agent cares about affordance.

1G   Store staff are there to ease the flow of goods through shelves and checkout counters.

2R   A fresh assortment of food is within easy reach of those who live close by; private stocks on public shelves.

3RT   The goods are available in a variety of sizes, packages, and grades; priced and labeled for retail purchase.

4GU   The store layout, signage, and displays make it easy to find what you are looking for and claim it for yourself.

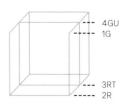

1G-2C-3CA-4UG in which the agent cares about performance.

1G   Store staff are there to ease the flow of goods through shelves and checkout counters.

2C   The store's checkout system converts recipes and shopping lists into bags of groceries.

3CA   Scanning an item transfers the ownership of the good to the bill the buyer is going to pay

4UG   Claiming those items at a store counter allows the cashier to process them for sale.

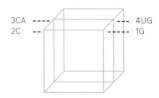

Weaving in the four supply-side narratives into the story completes it:

»Khairun enjoys a lifestyle and diet that keep her healthy, happy, and well within budget. Often, the Ottolenghi fan picks a recipe she likes and then gathers things to prepare the meal. Some recipes call for ingredients that make her *mise en place* set up incomplete. Not everything is at hand because she makes meals with fresh ingredients from a local store. As the retail end of supply chains, the store offers continuity in lifestyles and diets. A fresh assortment of food is within easy reach of those who live close by; private stocks on public shelves. The goods are available in a variety of sizes, packages, and grades; priced and labeled for retail purchase. Buying only what a recipe needs to have, when needed, is often better for the Planet, purse, and plate. Store

staff are there to ease the flow of goods through shelves and checkout counters. The store layout, signage, and displays make it easy to find what you are looking for and claim it for yourself. What is not in the kitchen is in the cart, within minutes of deciding what to make. Buying the ingredients and bringing them home is necessary to make the meal. Claiming those items at a store counter allows the cashier to process them for sale. The store's checkout system converts recipes and shopping lists into bags of groceries. Scanning an item transfers the ownership of the good to the bill the buyer is going to pay. When the items appear on a store receipt, the kitchen at home is soon replete; life goes uninterrupted.«

Design as code

Describing a service in 16 sentences by itself is neither difficult nor does it require a device like the 16x frame. But what we have here isn't just an ordinary description of how a grocery store serves a neighborhood. *It is an »executable script« with each sentence being a high-level declarative statement with design intent and guidance for the implementation.*[47] A script that every layer of the enterprise can read, interpret and execute in its own way for its own purpose – for example, to decide the location of the store, the assortment of goods, the layout and organization of the store, the staffing and training, the check-out process, and to drive the analytics for a keener understanding of lifestyles and habits.

Each layer has its own implementation-level detail separate from the script but linked to the statements. Therefore, one way to think about the script is that it is in hypertext: the statements are links or pointers to documents that store implementation-level details. For example, the 4UG and 4GU statements can point to different parts of a customer journey map, or any document detailing the design of the dialog and interaction between users and agents. This way, different parts of the design are in the files, styles, and formats that best communicate and capture the design, while the shared concept is in the format of the stories and 16x frames.

The detailed designs thus implement the 16 statements. New ideas have a basis for evaluation. Those that challenge or contradict a statement, prompt discussion. Changes to any one statement can cause changes to other statements and the entire story.

This makes the 16x frame the ground for achieving consensus between the layers of the enterprise – the stakeholders of the design.[48] The overall design of the service adapts and evolves over time, getting incrementally better as smaller and more specific changes lead to improvements, without inadvertently adding any new risk of systemic failure.

Figure 38
Design as code

	Y+	Y-	X+	X-	
who		▬		▬	1M
who		▬		▬	1U
why		▬			2A
why				▬	2T
who	▬		▬		1V
why			▬		2R
how			▬		3RT
how	▬		▬	▬	3TR
who	▬		▬		1G
what			▬	▬	4GU
what			▬	▬	4MV
how		▬			3AC
what	▬	▬			4UG
why		▬			2C
how	▬				3CA
what	▬	▬			4MV
	Y+	Y-	X+	X-	

Customer stories

Customers are equal stakeholders in the design of a service. Enterprises procure services for the benefit of hundreds and thousands of users at a time. Such procurement is a notoriously difficult job. The greater the contract value, the greater the possibility for hidden and unexpected costs. To protect themselves from the risks, customers and service providers add terms and conditions that act like uncertainty buffers. In doing so, they un-

FRAME, STORY AND SCRIPT

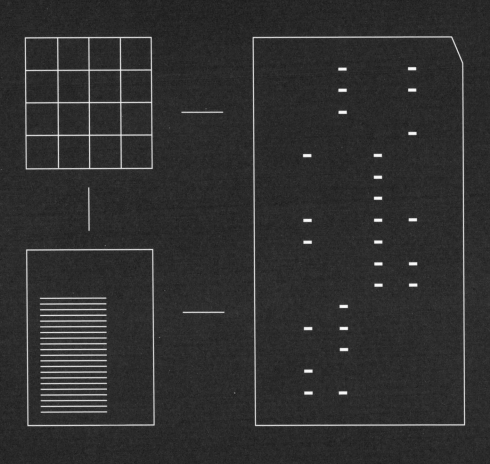

fortunately also add costs. Laws that govern public-sector procurement make it even more difficult, because of the commitments to a fair and transparent process, and the stewardship of taxpayer's money. Thus, the need for improving the tradecraft in the acquisition of services, and better buying power.[49]

The promises customers make (X-, Y-) are an integral part of the script. If customers are co-producers of value (Edvardsson, Gustafsson, Kristensson, Tronvoll, & Witell, 2014), it follows they can make changes to the script. If customer needs change, the script changes. If commitments change, the script changes. If customers do not play their part, the service fails to happen even though the potential may exist. In fact, customers may be the lead authors in many cases. Take the procurement of services under government rules, for example. »What exactly are we buying when we are buying a service?«

Procurement is often costly and cumbersome partly because of the language used. Stories from the 16x are then the basis for clarifying the buyer's intent in requests for proposals or invitations to tender. The bids and proposals then respond with stories of their own. It's better to first see which of those stories are most compelling, before diving into the details. Procurement officers can engage suppliers in a new kind of dialog that leads to better outcomes. The teams can then develop an entire set of 16x frames covering the customer journey in details. If customer needs change during the lifecycle of a contract, then »listening« to how the stories change is the best place to start.

Next, four 16x frames cover the rest of Khairun's day involving four other services. These four frames are an opportunity for you to practice story generation. You may have to edit the statements and through several iterations till the eight threads weave together well.

Payment processing ...

11:55

Khairun is now at a check-out counter with what she needs to prepare the meal. Once shoppers have what they need, making it easy for them to pay for their purchase and get back to the rest of their day is what the store promises. In the grocery business, a cumbersome check-out process is a major cause of dissatisfaction. Therefore, among other things, the store offers a contactless payment method. It procures from a payment service

1M customer	2A artifact	3AC task	4MV enhancement
For fast and easy check-out, the store offers shoppers several payment methods, for which it procures third-party services.	Khairun's ability to pay for her purchase, often in the form of a bank balance available through a debit card transaction.	A portion of the balance needs to be converted into a payment authorization for the store to receive funds for the purchase.	Khairun's ability to pay for the purchase is now verified and converted into a secure message that everybody can trust.
X -, Y -	Y -	Y -	Y +, Y -
2T event	**1U user**	**4UG commission**	**3CA activity**
The store simply wants surety on the pushing of an amount equal to what's on the receipt, from Khairun's bank account.	Paying the receipt total transfers ownership of the goods to the shopper, who prefers that step to be quick and easy.	Khairun submits her payment credentials by bringing her bank card in close proximity with the payment terminal.	The provider captures the transaction data and uses it to verify the validity of the card, and the availability of sufficient funds.
X -	X -, Y -	Y +, Y -	Y +
3TR access	**4GU provision**	**1G agent**	**2C capability**
The store needs to have from Khairun's bank a note that is as good as money, later in its own bank account.	The terminal indicates the status and progress of the card transaction, so Khairun and the store staff together know for sure.	The payment terminal initiates, coordinates, and completes the debit card transaction within seconds.	The provider has a PCI-compliant capture process for initiating the process for authorizing debit card payments.
X -	X +, X -	X +, Y +	Y +
4VM enrichment	**3RT availability**	**2R resource**	**1V provider**
The store's merchant bank account gets credited for the authorized amount, thus completing the purchase.	A message originating from the issuer bank, through a secure channel, confirms the store will receive the exact amount.	Point-of-sale infrastructure and secure access to data from payment processors allow it to issue payment authorizations.	The payment provider organizes card transactions to speed up the check-out process while reducing the risk of fraud.
X +, X -	X +	X +	X +, Y +

provider, an independent sales organization (ISO), the promise to speed up the check-out process while reducing the risk of fraudulent transactions.

As in the case of Alice getting to use Wi-Fi on the train as part of her ticket purchase, here we have an example of a service

Figure 39
11:55 Payment processing ...

in which a service provider is the customer and their customer is the user. There is a difference though. Alice's use of the Wi-Fi didn't clear the tracks or make the train go faster. Here the store (customer) and the shopper (user) are both equally interested in fast and secure payment because it affects the quality of the outcomes associated with the primary service. Shoppers like Khairun have the satisfaction of paying with their EMV chip cards, the store staff have a much better experience, and the store has far fewer coins and notes to handle at the end of the day. Payment services are perhaps the most widely used type of service because every other type of service calls upon them. No wonder the industry is huge and still expanding, especially with mobile payments and direct debit transactions. The possibilities for what you can pay for from where continue to expand, with encryption technologies putting the equivalent of PCI-compliant secure payment terminals on browsers and smartphones. [50]

Parking

12:00

The store pays for up to one hour of parking in the neighborhood, to make the shopping a bit more convenient and freer of anxiety and stress. The parking service is provided by a local enterprise that is under contract with the municipality. The parking lot next to the store is open to the public. You don't have to shop at the store to be allowed to park. However, the store contributes toward the cost. Printed on the shop receipt is a QR code coupon, the value of which depends on the amount the shopper spends at the store during that visit. The kiosk where they pay for parking scans the QR code and applies the discount. Alternatively, they can scan their store-issued bonus card and use their loyalty points to obtain a larger discount.

Parking services attach time to a location. They rent a spot for a certain period of time or vend time attachable to any available space within a zone or a lot; an array of parking spots. When drivers vacate a spot, they give up any remaining time when it is displayed on meters attached to a spot. If some other vehicle pulls into that spot, they receive a fortuitous discount. Some systems print a ticket with an expiration date and time to be prominently displayed on the dashboard of the vehicle. In theory, the same driver (or someone else) can use the remaining time on a separate occasion if that happens to be within the same time slot and zone or lot. But that rarely happens. Yet other systems simply create a ticket that attaches the procured time to a license

1M customer The store pays for up to one hour of public parking in the neighborhood, to make the shopping a bit more convenient. X -, Y -	**2A artifact** The license plate number uniquely identifies the vehicle to whomever it may concern in any public or private space. Y -	**3AC task** The license plate number of the vehicle needs to be attached to a valid session: parking time + zone number. Y -	**4MV enhancement** To parking enforcement officers, the vehicle appears to have parking rights and therefore does not attract a fine. Y +, Y -
2T event On average, shoppers at the store need about 40 minutes of parking time in the lot next door. X -	**1U user** Shoppers park their vehicles in the parking lot next to the store, which provides them easy access to the store entrance. X -, Y -	**4UG commission** Submit the license plate number of the vehicle, along with the zone number for the parking spot where the vehicle is parked Y +, Y -	**3CA activity** Registering the vehicle's license plate number within the zone and time-stamping it creates a valid parking session. Y +
3TR access Their vehicles need to have a parking spot convenient and safe for loading groceries, for the time they are inside the store shopping. X -	**4GU provision** The kiosk creates a token that assures the validity of the parking and allows the store staff to reimburse the shopper for up to an hour. X +, X -	**1G agent** A self-service kiosk at the store entrance registers the vehicles and activates a session to make the parking valid. X +, Y +	**2C capability** A time-keeping system registers vehicles within a parking zone or spot and tracks the remaining time in a session. Y +
4VM enrichment With their vehicles safely parked nearby, shoppers are more quickly inside the store shopping without anxiety or stress. X +, X -	**3RT availability** Sessions are available to any registered vehicle, in 1/4-hour increments, for a two-hour maximum, during the fixed hours. X +	**2R resource** Several areas in each neighborhood are set aside as parking spaces open to the public during fixed hours; area multiplied by hours X +	**1V provider** The municipality has given a local enterprise the license and authority to operate parking spots in public spaces. X +, Y +

plate number and zone or lot. Enforcement staff can verify the record on a hand-held device. Drivers can remotely add more time using a smartphone and an app (hand-held personal parking meters). Only that vehicle can then return to make full use of the privilege.

Figure 40
12:00 Parking

11:35

11:55

DAY IN THE LIFE OF
KHAIRUN

17:37

12:00

15:30

Time at a particular location, a set of GPS coordinates, is the underlying non-rival good: the use by one precludes simultaneous use by others. Everything that goes into the design of the service, including the pay station or the app, is based on how the service provider seeks to profit from the scarcity of the good. The nature of the business depends so much on the type of congestion and conflict within an urban area. More self-driving cars or more bike lanes? Better public transportation? Park anywhere across the city as part of a monthly subscription or daily pass? Khairun leaves the store with her bag of groceries, enters the parking lot, walks to the far corner of it, exits it through a gate, and crosses the street to reach home. Parking is a service she doesn't have much propensity for. She has a bicycle, takes the bus for longer distances, and occasionally calls a cab.

Khairun is sitting in a chair paying very close attention as she begins to grasp what's on high-resolution display in front of her. She is thinking to himself: »*The level of detail is astonishing!*« She is listening as Dr. Langedijk points to a particular nerve, which is the reason why she is suffering from pain in her lower back. They browse through the anatomical detail layer upon layer displayed on the screen in very high resolution, which her doctor is able to manipulate. It's like they are going through a storyboard someone has meticulously put together in time for their consultation. »*It is called a hanging protocol,*« the doctor explains, noticing the astonishment. It's how the images and their various views are arranged, in a way that allows medical teams to have really good discussions about a patient's health condition, and to develop a treatment plan, as they are doing now with a physiotherapist in the room.

The images are from the MRI scan Khairun went through the previous week. She was dreading it (not because she is claustrophobic), but the team in radiography conducted the procedure so well, including the way they prepared her, with the careful placement of coils to capture the image. They showed a lot of care toward their patient, knowing full well how it feels to be in such an enclosed space, being subject to an intense magnetic field, with the magnets making very loud noises as they go on and off. She was surprised to hear that the technicians put themselves through a mock procedure, every now and then, just to remind themselves about what it feels like to be inside. Now that's empathy.

The hanging protocol

15:30

1M customer	**2A artifact**	**3AC task**	**4MV enhancement**
Khairun is getting medical treatment at a local hospital that is providing her with care under a health plan. X -, Y -	It is not clear why there is acute pain in her lower back, which is causing her a lot of distress. Y -	Her back needs to be subject to an MRI scan to detect any abnormalities that may have emerged. Y -	Khairun's condition is captured in high resolution in a way that allows the doctor to digitally walk through, nerve by nerve. Y +, Y -
2T event	**1U user**	**4UG commission**	**3CA activity**
The plan includes a follow-up meeting during which doctor and patient need further insight to decide on the treatment. X -	As a neurologist, Dr. Langedijk is figuring out what is causing the pain so Khairun promptly gets the right medical treatment X -, Y -	Dr. Langedijk fills out a form to specify the anatomical detail she is seeking and why, along with notes from her consultation. Y +, Y -	A carefully controlled process scans the specific dermatomes, using coils to capture the signals from Khairun's lower back. Y +
3TR access	**4GU provision**	**1G agent**	**2C capability**
They need to have the images from the MRI to be able to discuss the problem with Khairun and advise her on the next steps. X -	The DICOM hanging protocol displays the images on PACS workstations in a way that facilitates the reading situation. X +, X -	Radiographers set up the scan to support the doctor's investigation and add the images to the patient's health record. X +, Y +	MRI scanning induces the body to produce millions of signals that pixelate tissue in images of extremely high resolution. Y +
4VM enrichment	**3RT availability**	**2R resource**	**1V provider**
New insight from the MRI leads to a decision that sets up Khairun to receive further care. X +, X -	The images are securely available across the hospital through the picture archiving and communication system (PACS). X +	Their facility has a 3-Tesla scanner generating images in a resolution good enough to investigate most health conditions. X +	The radiology department has the license and mandate to provide medical imaging as an intramural service for the system. X +, Y +

Figure 41
15:30 The hanging protocol

In terms of technological advance, we have come a long way from Röntgen's X-rays to the Siemens 7-Tesla whole body MRI scanner, and the Philips Lumify ultraportable ultrasound device plugged into a smartphone. Continuous and preventive care requires teams across specialties to collaborate across various points of care, through the sharing of electronic medical records (EMR), including medical images. Given the heavy workloads they often face and the need to more immediately attend to patients, it is important for teams to have easy access to those images on any display that is secure and private enough for protected health information (PHI). Picture archiving and communication systems (PACS) help make that possible. Combined with advanced informatics, automated workflows, and machine learning, imaging solutions are raising the bar on when and where what kind of care is delivered.

Khairun leaves the hospital quite satisfied with the treatment Dr. Langedijk and the team have proposed. She feels lucky to have such a fine doctor who goes through the pains to figure out what is causing the pain. Being a total geek, she is also wondering what the MRI scans from that 10.5-Tesla machine at the University of Minnesota look like, given that the magnetic field in that one is 10 times greater than that in a standard MRI scanner.[51] Right now though she needs to catch that bus to the polling station before it gets too late. She hasn't missed voting in an election in the last 48 years. She is not going to start today.

Khairun arrives at the polling station, feeling the same sense of empowerment she felt when she voted for the first time. She gets just one vote, like everybody else, but it's her vote. Not that she isn't cynical about the outsized influence of money in politics or the vagaries of vox populi. But she is also vehemently opposed to the apathy that leads some people to shirk from their duty. Besides, unlike the parking lot, this is a service she has already paid for with all those taxes. Now she is going to get what she paid for: the ballot, private access to the voting machine, and the assurance her vote will be counted toward the total.

The counting protocol

17:37

She is greeted by a volunteer who recognizes her from her unbroken voting record. Nevertheless, she has to identify himself with the voter identification card she received by mail. She has seen this ballot evolve over the years, through all sorts of formats. Today what's in front of her is a touchscreen interface that guides her through the process and captures her input. This MUJI fan loves the design, for not only what's been included but also for what's been left out. To her, the capacitive glass surface is still that »beautiful piece of paper« that, figuratively speaking, only a government knows how to print. As a retired civil servant,

1M customer	2A artifact	3AC task	4MV enhancement
To elect a government, taxpayers require the country to conduct free and fair elections.	The right includes the facility for their cast vote to be fully counted toward the final tally.	The recorded vote needs to be counted for it to have its final impact.	Khairun's right to vote is now fully exercised and has caused its own impact on the overall result.
X -, Y -	Y -	Y -	Y +, Y -
2T event	**1U user**	**4UG commission**	**3CA activity**
Every election is a valuable opportunity to influence the agenda and government of the country.	Residents would like to exercise their legal right to cast a vote in free and fair elections.	By marking the ballot and releasing it to the ballot box (voting machine), the voters submits their vote for counting.	Counting of the vote begins after the polls close and continues until the last ballot has been counted toward the total.
X -	X -, Y -	Y +, Y -	Y +
3TR access	**4GU provision**	**1G agent**	**2C capability**
The voter needs to have a legible, blank and intact copy of the ballot on which to record their vote.	Each eligible voter who arrives at the polling station during voting hours is handed the ballot.	Election officials supervise the operation to make sure everybody on the roll gets the opportunity to vote without difficulty.	The Board of Elections has a system for producing an accurate count of votes cast in an election, in accordance with the laws.
X -	X +, X -	X +, Y +	Y +
4VM enrichment	**3RT availability**	**2R resource**	**1V provider**
Khairun has the opportunity to have her say in the election in a way that actually counts toward the result.	The ballot is the »piece of paper« on which a personal opinion and political choice officially become a valid vote.	Its voter database maintains a list of citizens eligible and registered to vote in an election, in which there is public confidence.	The Board of Elections has the legitimacy and authority to conduct free and fair elections, without outside influence.
X +, X -	X +	X +	X +, Y +

Figure 42
17:37 The counting protocol

she knows something about that special pigment called public confidence that makes ordinary pieces of paper into something powerful; enough to turn the personal opinions of citizens into votes. Votes that can give governments a nasty paper cut if the services they provide do not produce the outcomes and impact they promised in the previous election.

A 2016 report, titled *The Public Impact Fundamentals Report*, found three components to be fundamental to public impact: *legitimacy, policy, and action* (CPI, 2016). The report defines legitimacy as follows:

»Legitimacy refers to the underlying support for a government or public body. Governments and bodies that are legitimate tend to be more successful in achieving impact. When it is absent, politicians are unable to draw on their mandate to push through initiatives. Legitimacy can also reduce the transaction costs of governing by reducing reliance on coercion and monitoring.«

The part about reducing transaction costs is particularly relevant to the design of services as a set of four promises. When transaction costs are too high, the promises become costly and cumbersome for both customers and service providers. Public confidence is an element of legitimacy and it refers to: »the extent to which the general public trusts institutions to act competently and in support of the wider public interest.« Therefore, in any 16x frame outlining the concept of a service, when the provider is a public-sector institution, public confidence is implicitly part of the resource (2R), and therefore the affordance.

It's been a long day for Khairun, but she is happy as she heads home.

Take two coffee tables

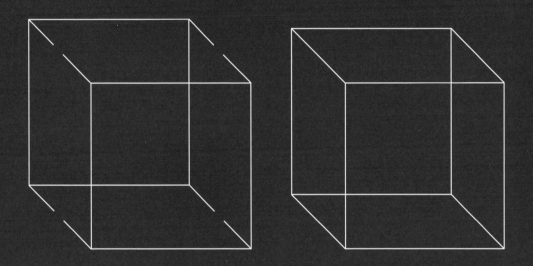

Set them on their sides   Join them at their feet

Part

Three

8

Tensions

8

The design of a service aims to keep both sides happy at the same time. From the customer's perspective, the service may disappoint because of the quality of outcomes and experiences, or the price may be too high. Any of those three reasons may make the service less attractive to a customer in terms of net value. Providers may feel the same based on their own net value calculations.

Even if customer needs by themselves aren't hard to fulfill, the actual instances of demand may be too costly to serve. Artifacts and events may be hard to handle. Users may be difficult to take care of; a lousy experience for the provider's agents. Therefore, while the price may be too high for customers, it may not be high enough from the provider's perspective.

Services can be a frustrating business to be in. Take for example some of the frustrations. »It takes too long, going from identifying the need to launching a new or improved service.« »It takes many layers to implement policy and strategy and it's hard to get everybody on the same page.« »There is distortion, noise, and error at every stage and layer. Everybody's got their own biases and blind spots.« »Ideation workshops create a lot of happy noise: People have fun but generate ideas we can't implement. We are a ring-fenced bank.« »The users of course are happy, but the customers are not. They feel they are paying too much.« »Choices feel like compromises.« »Customers no longer want X. They want X as a service, and we're figuring out what that means.« »The forecasts looked good, but the demand failed to show up.« »Customer satisfaction is at an all-time high. Of course, the budgets cuts will take care of that.« »We got blind-sided by a major failure.

The truth is, we weren't imaginative enough.« »It takes too long to figure out what the problem is. Then, when we fix it, things get worse!« »When the service doesn't fail, it often fails to excite. Failure has made us cautious while our customers ask what's new.«

These problems create tensions between customers and service providers along the lines of outcomes, experiences, and price. Some amount of tension is inevitable and may even be healthy. Too much of it, and the service may fail. The problem is not limited to commercial service providers. Governments and nonprofit organizations also face it, though their missions and mandates may allow them to accept lower net values, for the sake of public good. Let us understand the three tensions by revisiting the healthcare linen case.

The experiment

H is a healthcare system of general hospitals, clinics, and independent practices that is growing. That means they are caring for a larger population than before, which includes sicker and older patients. They are a privately-owned for-profit organization but with a founding philosophy that allows them to care less about their financial bottom line than they would otherwise have to. It doesn't mean they do not have to be mindful about their operating costs. It simply means, including in their bottom-line is social impact. Their business practices reflect that. They take care of their employees as they take care of their patients. They are also known to treat their suppliers well. *They believe an ecosystem of services is more sustainable in the long-term when it includes healthier financial statements.* They are systems thinkers to the core and not afraid to experiment now to develop instruments and methods for the future. All this in an industry in which services must meet the expectations of many organizations, stakeholders, providers, and users; in which the boundaries between people and things is ambiguous; and in which errors aren't just costly, they can be fatal.

The need

So far, it has made sense for them to own and operate their own laundry facility. An internal unit (W) has effectively supported their caregiving operations from having an intimate knowledge of their systems and methods. That was before they grew into a larger system, spreading across many more locations and offering more kinds of services, and therefore having more points of care at which linen becomes soiled. A few errors have been eye-opening, pointing to the fact that they may soon be at a tipping point, beyond which W may find it difficult to promise patients and staff the level of care they have in the past.

Major investments would be necessary to keep up with the growth, including technological upgrades, additional space in terms of prime real estate, and hiring more staff. That would still not solve the logistical problem of having to cover more locations than before. They would also have to invest in the delivery operation by adding drivers and vehicles. Therefore, the hospital decides to invest instead in a long-term relationship with a local service provider who can take over operational responsibility of the linen. H retains accountability for the overall safety and comfort of its staff and patients.

The hospital hires Q, an independent rating agency, specializing in the design of service contracts. The agency has a new method for evaluating the net value for customers and service providers. They use it to design contracts that pay off well for both customers and service providers. This assures the viability of a long-term relationship in which both sides buy into each other's success. That goes well with the hospital's policy of taking care of the ecosystem it depends on for its own success. That includes the welfare and wellbeing of local communities and businesses. Therefore, with respect to contracts that outsource an internal process and buy it as a service instead, there should be the same level of transparency and trust as with an internal unit.

A new method

The agency conducts an evaluation to find out what the hospital has been spending so far on taking care of the linen, and how much it would be willing to pay a service provider who is willing to take over the process. It presents its analysis in units called HEX. They relate the qualities of outcomes and experiences with the quality of price or payments. The idea is, experiences are price coefficients and therefore crucial determinants of net value. HEX help avoid making decisions based purely on price.

Every month, across five locations, the process of cleaning and sterilizing soiled linen, and ensuring patients and staff always have enough stock of clean linen, is worth 12000 HEX to the H mission. W gets it done internally on a monthly budget of 10000 HEX. The true cost of getting the job done is 11111 HEX, after accounting for coordination costs and management overheads. How much would outside service providers charge? Given the economies of scale and scope they tend to develop, and their greater appetite for assuming risks related to the core of their business, they would most likely offer to get the job done cheaper and probably better.

The three offers

External offers would have to be significantly lower than the internal benchmark for an important reason: transaction costs. Or, the sum of all the costs incurred in having a contract in place, achieving steady state for the outsourced operations, evaluating the outcomes and experiences, financial administration, resolving issues, and enforcing agreements. Those are the costs of simply being a customer, however fair, transparent, and equitable the customer may be. Therefore, upon Q's recommendation, H decides to be open to offers that promise a net value of at least 1000 HEX in terms of the mission impact. Three service providers, X, Y, and Z, respond to H's request for proposals, with the following offers:

X promises to get the job done for 10000 HEX
Y, for 11500 HEX
Z, for 9000 HEX

The offers from X and Y compare favorably against W, with the internal budget of 10000 HEX. Y seems more expensive. Which offer should H consider to be the best and why? This is where Q applies a system for evaluating service contracts based on net value.

The equation

O-P/E=N is an empirical equation that relates outcomes, experiences, and price or payments.

The O number indicates the quality of outcomes in terms of the gains (or avoided losses) that materialize from paying for or providing a service multiplied by the probability of realizing them within a timeframe. An outcome within the window of opportunity is worth more.

The P number indicates the quality of price or payment – price for customers and payment for providers – evaluated in terms of the amounts and timings. P incorporates the time value of the money – higher or lower amounts are acceptable against more favorable timings or cash flow.

The E number indicates the quality of experiences for users and agents during a fulfillment cycle. It is based on the levels of ease and effort they find while engaging each other in dialog and inter-action. E is the ratio of ease to effort.

O = (gains + avoided losses) * probability ... *quality of outcome*
P = (cost + fees) * timing ... *quality of payment or price*
E = ease/effort ... *quality of experience*
N = O-P/E ... *net value*

Outcomes – pricing/experience = net value

For example, for H, as a customer, the gains would be in terms of hospital staff and patients feeling more comfortable in their gowns, sheets, and scrubs from the linen being clean and fresh more of the time. The avoided losses could be in terms of avoiding feelings of discomfort, infections, and waiting time.[52] The probability of all that happening depends on how well the laundry cleans and sterilizes the linen (enhancement) and how quickly and completely they replenish the stocks (enrichment), within the windows of opportunity defined by the caregiving. Outside those windows, who cares? The probability is lower if the cleaning or sterilization are not as good, or if the clean linen isn't there as and when needed. The costs are what H would incur in getting the job by themselves. The fees are what they pay for someone else to assume the risks of those costs. The timing simply reflects the time value of money or the discounting of cash flows. For example, do they have to pay in advance, and yearly or monthly?

The ease refers to all that the hospital staff do not have to do or go through in using the service, because the laundry's agents take care of it, such as removing the soiled linen, replacing it with clean linen, and placing it where it is most needed. Ease includes the time the hospital staff do not have to spend waiting. The effort is what they do have to go through for the laundry staff to be able to get the job done well. That would include, for instance, deciding to change the linen, placing it in designated spaces (or not leaving it everywhere), signaling the agents, no matter how subtly, and »*helping themselves*« to the clean linen.

The laundry of course has its own expectations of earning net value. Below a certain point the business is unsustainable. They also have to worry about making gains that recover their long-term investments. They have to avoid loss in terms of idle capacity across their assets, including the workforce. Long-term contracts that involve regular payments, such as the one with H, would increase those probabilities. The payments customers make define the O numbers for services providers. The costs they incur and the fees they pay, define the P numbers. The ease and effort with which their agents engage with users at H, define their E numbers. How easy will the customers and users make it for their staff to have access throughout the hospital? What additional tasks do they assume responsibility for? What expectations do the users have of them? These and other questions have an impact on the laundry's net value.

Linking of net values

Both customers and providers would like their N value to be as high as possible. Here comes the tricky part. For customers, the P number represents what they are paying for the service. The P number for customers determines the O number for the service providers. Which means providers don't mind customers accepting a higher P number and returning them a higher O and N. But the price can't be too high for then it can push the N for customers below a threshold. Price can't be too low either, otherwise it could affect the provider's chances of recovering costs and covering their own payment obligations (e.g., to employees, suppliers, governments, and lending institutions). Poor financial health would then affect the quality of outcomes and experiences the provider can sustain. Customers like H don't want their suppliers and partners to face financial stress, wary of the risk to their own operations. This is where the E number plays an important role in reducing tension.

Experience as the cost coefficient

Customers and service providers both receive E-ratings, giving them the basis to negotiate better experiences for their users and agents. For a given set of values of O and P, the net value for service providers will be higher if customers have a higher E rating. The net value for customers will similarly be higher when users have better experiences. That is the reason why E divides P in the equation. For customers, when E > 1.0, then it has the effect of a discount on the payments and the net value is better than expected. When E < 1.0, then it has the effect of a penalty or surcharge, and the net value is less than expected. There is a shifting of the burden from agents to users.

The E-ratings of customers similarly apply. The quality of experience matters as much for the employees and agents of the service provider. And it matters because the levels of ease and effort that agents experience have an impact on the provider's net value. When E < 1.0 it means that users are harder to deal with and require more effort on part of the agents than expected. There is a shifting of the burden in the direction of the agents. What service providers typically do is to anticipate the additional costs, create a cost buffer, and price it into their offers. Or, impose terms and conditions to control behaviors. But that can be counterproductive, as we shall see.

The higher the E number, the better the quality of the experience. The design of a service could be such that users and agents engage each other in ways that produce higher quality experiences for each other, or a higher E number. For the offers made by X, Y, and Z the E numbers are as follows:

X, 0.95
Y, 1.05
Z, 0.85

To make the evaluations fair and complete, Q has conducted an analysis about the quality of experience W has so far offered. Based on interviews with hospital staff and internal records from the H organization, it has assigned it an E number of 0.9. That compares favorably with Z, while X and Y promise to offer a higher quality of experience.

H expects all three offers to yield a net value of 1000 HEX or more. Applying the formula to each of the three offers allows Q to make the following calculations of the net values the three service providers may be able to produce on a monthly basis, and therefore the attractiveness of their offers in the long term:

Comparing the three offers

X's offer,
O = 12000, E = 0.95, P = 10000
[Offering same O and P as W, but a better E]
N = 12000 - 10000/0.95
N = 1474 HEX

Y's offer,
O = 12500, E = 1.05, P = 11500
[Offering better O and E than W, but a higher P]
N = 12500 - 11000/1.05
N = 1548 HEX

Z's offer,
O = 11500, E = 0.85, P = 9000
[Offering worse O and E than W, but a lower P]
N = 11500 - 9000/0.85
N = 912 HEX

For W, the Do-It-Yourself (DIY) option,
O = 12000, E = 0.90, P = 10000
N = 12000 - 10000/0.90
N = 889 HEX

The evaluation

On price alone, the offer from Z seems to be significantly cheaper than W or DIY. However, after factoring in the quality of outcomes and experiences, X and Y seem to have superior offers in terms of net value. Both are significantly better than W, whereas Z is simply not. Z is ruled out as an option for the following reason. While they promise to get the job done as well as W has done, their quality of outcomes is actually lower. That is because they are unable to offer the exchange cart delivery option, which would significantly improve the affordance in terms of the hospital staff having stacks of clean linen from which they can more quickly grab and go. X and Y both offer that, and the hospital staff love the idea. As users of the service, it will make things easier for them, and their managers care about that. They don't mind spending a bit more on that. That's the consensus. While not offering that option allows Z to offer a lower price, it also affects their E number. While W didn't offer exchange carts either, their staff being an integral part of the H organization with access to all areas, could personally fetch the linen from the clean closet and bring it to their colleagues, if necessary.

During internal discussions, which included key management and staff within W, the procurement team weighs in with a recommendation in favor of accepting the offer from X for the following reasons. They offer a net value that is significantly higher than the threshold criterion of 1000 HEX. They do so by matching the O and P values for W, while improving upon the quality of experience for the hospital staff. Of course, Y promises an even higher net value. They are able to do so because of a more advanced washing technology, a larger installed capacity that is almost twice that of X, and data analytics that could provide new insights into operations. However, the H team didn't foresee that much advantage from those differences. They were eyeing the E numbers instead. If X can be motivated to improve E number by a few basis points, the net value their services produce will approximate that which Y is offering.

Therefore, they decide to award X an initial 3-year contract with the following stipulation. Every six months, Q would conduct evaluations to ensure the N from X does not fall below 1400. That would give X some latitude, given the inherent risks in the demand for linen from across the H system, while protecting the interests of hospital staff with respect to the linen. If X were to achieve N=2000, they would receive a bonus payment of 500 HEX per month, for that period. The decision was partly influenced by a system-wide drive to improve the quality of experiences for H staff from supporting services. By specifying a +/- range for N, instead of insisting on a point target, H believed they would promote healthy tension, which would encourage X to truly understand the experiences of their staff and patients.

All three providers were eager to win the contract, given the reputation H has for developing long-term relationships and treating their suppliers like partners. They took into consideration the quality of outcomes and experiences, and the price necessary to promise and deliver the net value the H company considered worthwhile. And while being in the same business meant that each provider had more or less similar capabilities and resources, they perceived different levels of costs and risks in fulfilling demand from H. Each looked at the opportunity from the perspective of their own net values. Based on Q's published ratings, the E number for H is known to be 0.90.

The decision

X, Y, and Z

Applying O-P/E=N to get an indication of N values for providers:

N for X,
O = 10000, P = 8750, E = 0.90
N = 10000 - 8750/0.90
N = 278 HEX

N for Y,
O = 11500, P = 10000, E = 1.05
N = 11500 - 10000/0.90
N = 389 HEX

N for Z,
O = 9000, P = 8000, E = 0.85
N = 9000 - 8000/0.90
N = 111 HEX

Each approached the H opportunity with an offer that reflected not only their strategy and operations, but also their contracts with other customers. They have to optimize their designs to work well for all of those contracts. From each contract they earn net value. Not all of those other contracts measure net value in terms of HEX. At some level, what might be attractive to one of their customers may not be as attractive to another. Therefore, their offers reflected the way most of their other customers make purchasing decisions.

Z is a company that has found success as a low-cost service provider to smaller and more price-sensitive customers, who do not mind the lower E numbers. Compared to X and Y, Z is a »low-fare laundry« offering a no-frills service. They expect their customers to accept certain inconveniences, pay more in advance, and put in more *effort* through »self-service«.

Y caters to the higher end of the market, catering for large-scale operations with exacting standards that are willing to pay a premium. Therefore, Y has optimized their designs to deliver higher net values at higher prices. And therefore, they are always pushing the envelope in terms of their technology, such as advanced washing, data analytics, and being the first ones to offer exchange delivery carts.

X largely caters for the middle of the market. They started as a

very small operation and had to make major upgrades to be able
to meet the commitments of their first large contract. There were
growing pains and their management philosophy tends to heavily
emphasize lean operations. They've learned from their past mis-
takes of aggressive cost-cutting, the predictable consequences
of which were operational failures and customer dissatisfaction.
They embarked upon a careful study of how to better implement
the division of labor between users and agents, keeping in mind
the particular needs of operating environments in larger enterprises. As a result, they were able put together a winning bid.

While prices can remain fixed, net value can still vary. Several
transactions define the timescale of a contract, and a series of
contract renewals may define the relationship. Both sides would
like to nurture relationships that pay off well over time. *Relationships are reassuring.* Apart from avoiding the costs of switch-
ing and setting up new contracts, they accumulate goodwill and
trust that go far in mitigating risks and reducing costs per transaction. In the first two years, X surpassed the net value targets
defined in the contract and profited from their audacious bet. H
decided to extend the contract by another three years. Meanwhile, they also won contracts from other hospitals based on
their success at H. They also expanded into the hospitality industry after winning a contract with a major hotel. Meanwhile, H
continued to experience significant growth.

Three years later

The Chief Financial Officer (CFO) at X has been tracking their N
values. Here is what she saw. The very timely payments from the
H contract amounted to a very good quality of outcome for X.

At the start of year 1:

O = 10500 ... including the bonus payment from H
P = 8875 ... including additional costs to ramp up their E
E = 0.9 ... the E rating of H users as experienced by X agents
N = 639

From the CFO's perspective, this looked very good. The additional
375 HEX (spread over three years) they put toward improving the
H user experience from E = 0.95 to 1.05 was paying off to the tune
of 361 HEX, due to the bonus payment. Otherwise, the N value
would have been 278 HEX. That was in no small part due to H hav-

ing a policy in the first place that so explicitly rewarded service providers for delivering superior sets of experiences. Of course, with X producing a much higher quality of experience (E = 1.05), as a customer H was enjoying a much higher net value, at N = 2000. That increase was in fact covering the bonus. The Q system seemed to go well with their own philosophy and management style.

In the third year, things started to noticeably change. For the first time ever, the N values that X was producing missed the bonus target, even though they didn't fall below the lower threshold of 1400 HEX. The expanded user base led to situations in which some users were very happy and others not so much. Soiled linen was piling up in new patterns. To cope with the added demand, X decided to hire a subcontractor to handle the pick-up and delivery of linen. That didn't help at all. Meanwhile, two smaller hospitals acquired by H were added to the contract. Their expansion brought in new care settings and treatments that significantly changed the nature of the demand X had to now engage with, especially the user base.

By the middle of the third year:

O = 10500 ... barely made the bonus target
P = 8950 ... including payments to the subcontractor
E = 0.87 ... H user base getting more difficult to serve
N = 213 ... below expectations, but still not bad

By the middle of the fourth year, things became difficult for X as they tried hard to keep the net value for H at 1500 or above. H could see a noticeable difference in their E numbers, which fell to 0.95. The staff at X, both those at the laundry facility and those deployed in the hospital, were feeling a lot more stress.

O = 10000 ... missed the target; no bonus
P = 8975 ... operations already lean; X can't cut costs further
E = 0.91 ... getting adjusted to the expanded user base
N = 110 ... much lower net value for X than expected

Analysis

X seems to have fallen into a vicious cycle, triggered ironically by their own success and that of their customer. Their success at H in the first two years encouraged them to accept the contract renewal, even though the user base there was about to change. The changes in the quality of demand made it much more difficult for them to continue to meet it as before. Their other contract wins meanwhile stretched them thin once again. They could cut costs only to the extent that there was waste. But if the operations were already quite lean, further cost-cutting could affect the quality of outcomes and experiences, resulting in lower N values for customers. In response, customers could either pay less, use less, or simply take their demand elsewhere. That might leave service providers worse off than before. X tried to keep hitting the net value targets and maintain its reputation by absorbing the costs, since the payments were fixed. However, that reduced the net values they enjoyed. In reality, the subsequent instances of demand were simply costlier to serve, and given the nature of the contract in place, they were unable to charge extrato recover the additional costs. While the H contract had incentives for X surpassing the net value targets, it didn't account for scenarios where X's operating costs went up because of changes in the user base.

Figure 43
Empathy chart

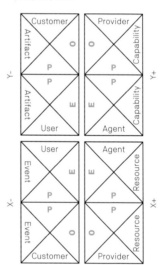

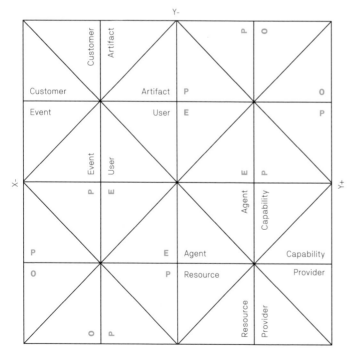

The trade-offs

There is a difference between a service failing to produce the outcomes and failing to produce the experiences. Take for example someone who needs to be at a particular place on a particular day within a particular hour. If they can be there on time, they stand to gain something or avoid a loss. That outcome is therefore worth $ 1500 to them. Let's say that $500 is their prospective gain, and $ 1000 is their prospective loss because they have already purchased tickets for a special concert that day. The problem is, the destination is 2000 miles away. Therefore, they are willing to pay up to $ 1000 for a seat on a nonstop flight that will get them there on time, because it departs and arrives within particular time slots (affordance) and the aircraft flies at speeds of over 550 miles per hour (performance).

An alternative way of getting there would cost the traveler $ 250, but with a very low chance of being there on time. Or, it may cost them a considerable amount of time and energy to get there on their own. They'd rather pay $ 1000 for the nonstop flight, framing the additional amount as the airline's fee for flying them there on time, instead. The fee is $ 750 and not $ 75000 because »a hundred« other passengers are also sharing the ride, some of them paying far more and others paying far less. Why? Because each one has their own reason for being on that flight, and their own perception of what the exact same outcome is worth. That makes a difference, along with perhaps the timing of their purchase. Tickets tend to be cheaper when purchased in advance.

The airline has a record of producing on-time arrivals 95% of the time. Which means that, already, the expected value of the outcome is O = $ 1425. The passengers may have paid for the ticket using a method that costs them 5% of the amount, including the processing fees, and accrued interest from having made an advanced purchase. So, the trip is already costing them P = $ 1050. Even before they leave for the airport, the net value the service will produce is likely to be closer to N = $ 375 than $ 500. The passenger has so far only procured the privilege of occupying a seat on that flight. They now have to put in the effort to board the plane. That could mean anything from »Oh, that was so easy, what a wonderful experience!« to »Oh my god! That was a painful process.« For simplicity's sake, let's ignore the effort involved in making the journey to the airport. That is beyond the control of the airline and the airport.

The check-in, security, and boarding processes constitute ef-fort, largely due to the possibility of queues at every stage. Also, if the airline operates its flights out of a particular terminal and the aircraft gets assigned a particular gate, passengers have to put in additional effort. That is particularly difficult when young children, the elderly, or the pregnant are involved. However, the airline and its agents (including the airport) put in a counter-bal-ancing effort to make it all easier for their passengers.[53] That in-cludes the speed and convenience they design into the check-in and boarding processes, including special assistance for those who request it.

To sum up, all the effort the airline (and airport) put in, amounts to the ease for the passengers. It is difficult to measure, but rat-ings are often given on a 1-10 scale. For the passenger paying $ 1500 to fly to (San Francisco?), let's say we can assign the surro-gate value of ease = 7.0. The balance is left to the passenger. Let's say that value is effort = 8.0. Ease and effort together result in a quality of experience, E = 0.875.

Therefore, applying the equation,

net value = (gains + avoided losses) * probability − (costs + fees) * timing/(ease/effort)
$N = (500 + 1000) * 0.95 − (100 + 900) * 1.05 / (7.0/8.0)$
$N = 1425 − 1020/0.875$
$N = 225$

Competing on E

Factoring in the experience reduces the net value to 225 from a potential value of 375. Let's say for argument's sake that the airline is almost always on time and has a 99% rating. Then the net value increases to 285, which is why some people consider it worthwhile to pay a bit more to fly with airlines that have a reputation for being reliable. Similarly, if the airline designs its services such that passengers experience a lot more ease and a lot less effort, then the quality of the experience increases. Let's say in this case that ease and effort both have a rating of 10.0. Then E = 1.0 and the net value increases to N = 435, or 375 with 95% on-time arrival. That's the net value impact of the quality of experience. Again, that makes sense. Airlines attract customers, not just on the basis of when they can fly them and where, but also on the basis of the quality of experience they offer throughout the journey. That strategy can result in fuller flights with higher fares.

For that particular flight, the net value equation for the airline could look like this:

$$N = (850 + 50) * 1.00 - (750 + 150) * 1.2/(8.0/7.0)$$
$$N = 1000 - 1080/1.14$$
$$N = 55$$

Fare game   The $ 900 the passenger paid for the ticket can be broken down into an $ 850 gain and a $ 50 avoided loss (cost of flying an empty seat) for the airline. And since it is a non-refundable fare with penalties for change, we can assign a probability of 1.0. The airline has to cover its costs and pay all sorts of fees for airport services, baggage handling, maintenance, and repair. Let's say that all of that adds up to $ 900. We apply a timing factor of 1.2 to account for the fact that those costs are not only incurred a long time in advance, sometimes months ahead, but have to be paid even if the aircraft flies half-empty (load factor). Airlines go to great lengths not just to make things easy for passengers, but also for themselves. Which is why they enforce certain rules. The effort passengers put in makes things easier for the airlines. Assuming ease = 8.0, and effort = 7.0, the quality of experience of the airline agents = 1.14. The number varies across passengers and across the classes of fare.

The airline puts in a lot more effort toward passengers traveling in business class and first class cabins, but that is more than compensated for by the premiums those passengers pay. The airline has to make additional arrangements that cater especially for those passengers, who are then also allowed to make last-minutes changes that could lead to empty seats. But other operating costs remain largely the same and are spread across all the classes of travel. We tweak the numbers just to illustrate the difference:

$$N = 3000 * 0.95 - 1500 * 1.25/(7.0/10.0)$$
$$N = 2850 - 1080/0.7$$
$$N = 171$$

Even though it is costlier to serve the premium fares, the airlines earn much higher net values from them. In many cases, the net value from a single first-class seat can make the difference between a flight being profitable or not. What about low-fare airlines then?

The low-fare airline

Low-fare airlines operate out of less expensive airports, thus transferring some of the costs to passengers, many of whom have to travel further to the airport. The facilities they provide are leaner, and the procedures they require passengers to follow are longer. They purchase time slots that are cheaper for them but tend to be during off-peak hours. They operate out of terminals and gates for which airports charge less of a premium. Some of them do not provide the convenience of a jet way, requiring passengers to ride a bus and climb stairs. Most importantly, they unbundle the legacy airline package. Passengers pay separately for seats, bags, meals, and in-inflight entertainment. Therefore, only the air fare is low. For a low-fare airline we can illustrate the difference with the following numbers:

$N = 350 * 1.0 - 500 * 1.1/(10.0/6.0)$
[Passenger fare: $ 275, seat: $ 25, bags: $ 50]
$N = 350 - 550/1.7$
$N = 20$

If the total cost of flying a passenger is $ 550 then how does applying the E factor magically make the costs disappear? $ 550 is the cost the airline would incur if it actually carries out all the effort that it passes on to passengers, who willingly accept the additional burdens in return for the low prices, including paying for travel to secondary airports at far off locations. Take a trip to make a trip. *Outcomes are what they pay for. Experience is what they pay with.*

When a flight is delayed

Take for example, an airline experiencing technical difficulties that are not attributable to weather or any such event outside their control. As a consequence, the flight arrives at the destination two hours late. The check-in and boarding experiences for all the passengers are otherwise great, and the bags arrive on time at the carousels. The airline of course apologizes for the delay, but if passengers and bags have safely reached their destinations, has the service really failed? And if so, in what way?

The airline prices its fares not just for the distance traveled (performance) but also for flying within two time slots (at origin and destination airports) on a particular day. If the flight is not on time, then the quality of outcomes produced is not the same as promised. In general, people pay to travel because they want to be somewhere sooner, and for longer. Losing time at the destination can be a real loss. The loss could feel even more frustrating if they had earlier given up the option of a much cheaper flight, that now would have arrived at the same time as the costlier one. So how do airlines get away with such delays?

Individuals have a tolerance for delay that varies from person to person on any given day. To some passengers the delay may not matter because it does not materialize into significant losses on that particular day. But for others it may. They may miss a connecting flight and then have to wait at the airport for what might be an even longer journey than it would have been before. While some airlines may offer compensation to maintain goodwill and trust, others don't.[54]

Djakarta via Djibouti

Django is a wildcatter from Texas. He wants to go to Djakarta. He refuses to consider some airlines because of the N values they return. They're too unreliable. He does a price search on Hipmunk, an online travel company that ranks flights not just by the usual criteria, but also the level of agony or pain (E number). Django finds, for the same class of travel, the nonstop options cost significantly more than the 1-stop ones, which are even more expensive than the 2-stop safaris. All the options arrive in Djakarta within the same hour. Django argues that the nonstop flight should be the cheapest one since on it he is flown the fewest miles, and that is less work for the airline.

Airlines are watching their N number for every flight. The airline is betting that there will be enough people who can bring them very high O numbers because they want to travel between a pair of time slots. Putting as many of them together as possible on the same flight would get them that big O they need to stay profitable. It's better for them to try and fly the rest to a hub, pack them tighter in fewer flights, or fly them with codeshare partners. Django isn't winning that argument because there are others willing to pay a lot more to be on that nonstop flight, unlike Django. There are also those with high thresholds for pain, and low thresholds for gain, unlike Django. They are happy to fill up more of the flight and get a step closer toward their final destination.[55] As airlines seek to maximize revenue per available seat-mile, every flight is a mix of those willing to *pay more for less* pain, and those who *pay less for more*, because they have a greater tolerance.

In many cases, it is difficult to give exact numerical values to the three variables. What is an outcome really worth? What is easy for one person could be too difficult for another. How do we precisely measure the level of ease or effort? What is the cost of the do-it-yourself option when it is almost impossible to do it yourself? What is a reasonable fee? It can all be very subjective. However, the cases in which we have a pretty good sense of what those numbers could be can serve as useful analogies with questions such as:

»What is our equivalent of the kiosk or counter?«
»Would our customers be willing to take a trip to make a trip?«
»What is the 'time slot' in our business?«

O-P/E=N

N=O-P/E

9

Tactics

9

**For customers and for providers, a higher N value means a supe-
rior set of outcomes and experiences at the lowest possible cost.
Since the net values for the two sides are linked to each other, an
increase in value for one side might be at the expense of the other,
thus setting up the three tensions. The three tensions vary from
market to market. They are the basis of strategy and design.**

**Strategy and
design**

Every service offering is based on pair of net values – one for the
customer (N_m) and one for the provider (N_v). In a given market,
the design of a service has the potential to generate a range of
net values. Which values are attractive, which are not, depends
on who is looking at them. Each side independently evaluates.
Both sides have thresholds for N. For customers, below a lower
threshold (M1) the net value is NOT OK. Above an upper threshold
(M2) it is GREAT. Between the two thresholds it is OK. Similarly,
service providers have similar thresholds (V1, V2) and similar sentiments about their net value being above, below, or in between
them. Therefore, when one side rejects an offer, the other side
understands. The three sentiments on the two sides give us nine
scenarios. When the N_m and N_v are both red (below lower thresholds), there is little or no possibility of agreement. When they are
both blue (above upper thresholds), the possibilities are great.
There are various other possibilities in between.

Figure 44
Transactional Analysis

Great ———
Ok   -------
Not ok ———

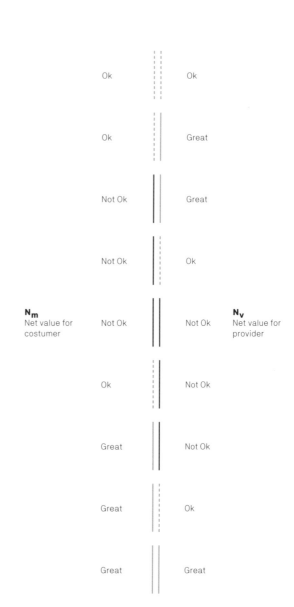

N$_m$
Net value for
costumer

N$_v$
Net value for
provider

Cooperation, conflict, and compromise

The linking of net values sets up the potential for cooperation, conflict, and compromise along two planes. When the two sides cooperate, they may arrive at a good compromise. *Good compromises are changes to the design of a service from which both sides are better off in the long run even if one of them is at a slight disadvantage at first.* Bad compromises are changes from which one side gains mostly at the expense of the other. A significant reduction in the net value for one side can trigger a vicious cycle, at the end of which both sides are worse off. Sooner or later the two sides may find themselves in unintended conflict. If there is enough choice in the market in terms of other sources of supply or demand, the relationship may break.

On the other hand, there may not be much choice. Customers may find themselves forced to pay for and make use of a service even at low N_m. Similarly, providers may accept low N_v for extended periods of time. An entire industry may accept lower prices because of competition. A challenger or new entrant may shake things up by offering higher net value at a lower price. They may be able to do that because of a genuine breakthrough in design. Or, they may do it simply to attract demand, taking a loss to consolidate market share and defeat competition, before making moves toward better returns. In many markets the winner takes all. An entire industry sector may feel compelled to raise prices due to changes in their operating environments, including new rules and regulations. Those costs are either to be absorbed or passed on to customers. The entire range of N values may shift for all customers buying from that sector.

In the public sector, the need to keep services affordable for all often forces service providers to accept low net values. Also, they may be reluctant to raise prices or restricted from doing so. Which is why we have services that only governments are willing to provide. *However, if we don't measure strictly in financial terms, public sector net values are actually quite high after accounting for goodwill, loyalty, and trust.* This is also true of service providers such as credit unions, cooperatives, communes, and faith-based organizations.

In a given market space, the design of a service can generate a range of net values – N_m and N_v – based on various combinations of O, P, and E on both sides. But there are nine pairs of reference values that define goal posts for the design. Each indicates the quality of design either in its current state, or a target for a future state based on a product strategy and roadmap. The reference values are useful for framing new ideas and evaluating their significance and impact through the lens of strategic design.

Reference values

»Strategy is a devised
course of action – the most
prudent path – toward
higher net values for both
sides. Therefore, strategy
is design.«

For example, »*Implementing ‹proposed feature› will help us get from ‹current position› to ‹target value›, because certain younger customers are then more likely to upgrade to the premium subscription*«. Or, they can be useful for grooming a product backlog by prioritizing ideas based on the part of a strategic plan they help implement.

Changes to the design of a service cause the net value pairs to move from one goal post toward another. Each change is in terms of the qualities of outcomes (O), prices or payments (P), or experiences (E), backed by one or more of the four promises. Like vectors, each movement can be further resolved into changes in gains, avoided losses, probabilities, costs, fees, timing, effort and ease, on either side (N_m or N_v).

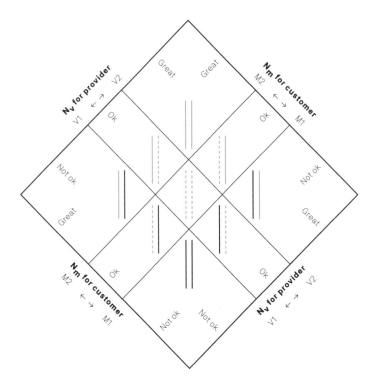

Figure 45
Empathy graph

——— Great
-------- Ok
——— Not ok

We can evaluate the design of a service by the net values it dependably produces.

Quality of design

Design that produces net values above the lower thresholds – M1 and V1 – is good design. Design that puts them above the upper thresholds – M2 and V2 – is great design. Such design is likely to have evolved over time through many sets of outcomes, experiences, and prices to reach an optimal state, with both sides challenging each other to offer something better.

The design of a service can be suboptimal but satisficing.[56] The customer or service provider could ask for more but is happy enough with a net value that is below their upper threshold (M2 or V2) but above the lower one. Many service designs end up in this area and stay there because customers and service providers are trading off over O, P, and E – by giving up a little of one to receive a little more of another.

Figure 46
Empathy graph,
quality of design

Great ———
Ok ------
Not ok ———

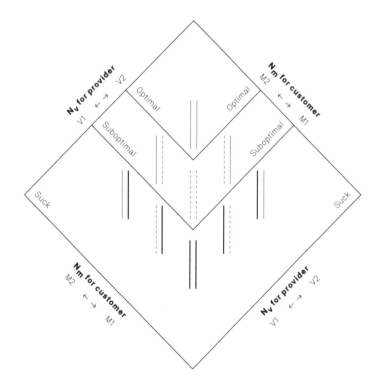

The design of a service may suck from the perspective of the customer or the service provider, or both. Customers may be unhappy but service providers aren't having too much fun either.

Yet they may be willing to accept offers for various reasons including those discussed earlier. Or, it might be that the net values suck only during a transitional period after which they return to a better normal. The situation may be acceptable for a while. Contracts that forcibly keep one side in a highly inequitable position for too long are prone to failure.

Every movement has a vertical and a horizontal component. The horizontal component of the movement represents a compromise, or the concessions between the pair of net values. The vertical component represents an increase or a decrease in net value. Compromises are good as long as they leave at least one side better off than before. *A series of good compromises result in an upward trend leaving both sides better off. A series of bad compromises result in downward trend that leaves both sides worse off.*

Tactical moves

Customers' needs change, as do providers' abilities to fulfill them. Service providers adjust to new realities by making changes to their designs that implement tactical moves within a market segment, competing on either outcome, experience, or price. Or, they may make a more calculated move with changes to two or three of the numbers at once mindful of the feedback loop between the net values. Customers in each segment may respond differently to N values from particular combinations of O, P and E. What's acceptable for one segment may not be for another. Developing a stronger position with respect to one segment, might open up weaknesses with respect to another.

A lateral shift of the pair values toward the left or the right signifies a change in equity or balance. Moves toward the middle lead to more equitable positions, with both sides being equally better off or worse off than before. Moves away from the middle reduce the balance and equity, leaving either the customer or the service provider in a position of disadvantage. Increase in the competition, or scarcity of demand or supply, can favor one side over the other. Even though the linking of net values forces mutual consideration, it's possible that one side has a greater advantage. Whether such an advantage is sustainable, depends on the outlook of the other side. *Are they making concessions as part of a plan, or are they the plan?*

WE CAN EVALUATE $\longrightarrow$ THE DESIGN OF A SERVICE

$\downarrow$

IT DEPENDABLY PRODUCES. $\longleftarrow$ BY THE NET VALUES

In his book *Obliquity* (2011), economist John Kay explains why some goals are best achieved indirectly, whether one is pursuing profit or personal happiness: because all such pursuits must take into account the interests of others who have a positive influence on your success. The same can be said of customers and service providers cooperating with each other and making a series of good compromises. Every path has risks, but some moves may be less stressful than others, with a lower danger of sliding downwards. Strategy is a devised course of action – a series of tactical moves towards a better position.

Consider the case of an existing service that over time has failed to create enough value for customers and service providers in one of the segments of the market space. It's in the red on both sides. There is a decline in new customers signing up for the service. The service provider first makes changes to the design to improve the user experience, leading to improvements in net value for customers, without having to reduce prices. The margins for the service providers remain dismal, but they manage to stop the churn and stabilize the demand. Also, while the improvements to the design have required costly investment, they are rolled out on top of an engagement platform that is common across other segments, including customers who pay premium prices.

Over time the troubled segment shows signs of growth. The increase in demand, combined with gradual cost savings from a simplified process, then brings the provider's net value above the lower threshold. The implementation of the tactic has proven to be successful. For the next few periods, the provider patiently waits as the segment enjoys the higher net values, contributes to revenue growth, and replenishes the once-depleted strategic reserves of goodwill and trust. At this point, the service provider makes a move to further improve their net values in this segment, and to consolidate their position within the market space. They could, for example, make changes to further improve user experience while at the same time using self-service options to make the division of labor more in their favor. That may require a very sophisticated design and careful implementation, to avoid shifting too much burden to users, which would result in a drop in the net values for customers. The improved user experience should make customers more eager to use the service, more often. The resulting increase in propensity and willingness to pay

Upward spiral

should support a small increase in price, resulting in a further improvement in the net value for the provider.

Figure 47
Upward spiral

Great ——
Ok ·······
Not ok ——

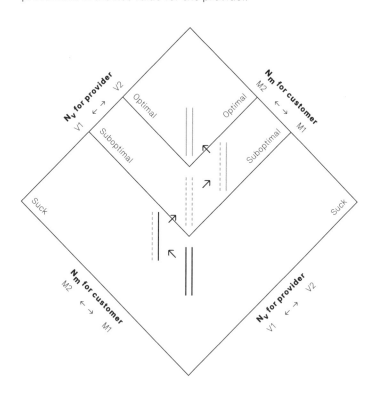

The balance is now in favor of the service provider. At this point, their net values are above the upper threshold. For customers, they are between the thresholds, and satisficing. The provider can declare success and enjoy the net values, having made the slow and steady climb to take net values from the undesirable region, to the acceptable. Or, they could take an even more long-term view. Every market space has its own internal dynamics. Customer needs change and competition can come from unlikely spaces. If net values for customers suddenly drop, there is the risk of slipping back toward the center, or worse, into the inequitable region. It may be better to further improve the design so customers enjoy a higher quality of outcomes, for example because of new and exciting content in a video on-demand catalog. The final move would make the quality of design optimal and take net values on both sides above the thresholds.

Every now and then an entirely new kind of service is born. The propensities lie beneath the surface. Customers aren't even fully aware of the needs until a service provider has the audacity to suggest them. The willingness to pay for a service is therefore initially low. Net values on both sides are below the thresholds. *Demand exists only in the imagination of supply.* Service providers have to develop service offerings that help create new habits and incorporate new kinds of absent assets, outcomes, and experiences into the daily lives and routines of customers and their things.

The hook

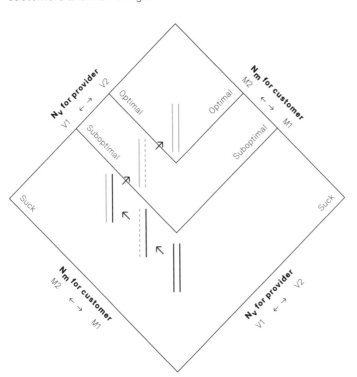

Figure 48
The hook

——— Great
------- Ok
——— Not ok

The design of the service offering needs to most definitely produce high-quality outcomes and experiences (O and E numbers). Customers may pay little or nothing for the service until they've used it long enough to first develop a liking for it, and then habits. The strategy then is to continuously improve the design to gradually increase net values for customers until they cross both thresholds. The net values for providers will have to remain in the red. When absent assets start to make their presence felt, it is time to introduce premium offerings for which a large enough percentage of customers are willing to pay. In some cases, the service provider may make the service a multi-sided platform, bringing together an entirely different segment of customers who are willing to pay for access to the originating segment. Thus, begins the steady climb toward the middle, higher net values for both sides. The design may allow for the possibility of freemium, through which one segment of customers effectively subsidizes another. In such cases, the strategy is to leave one pair of net values deliberately inequitable and unbalanced, in favor of another segment. Another pair of net values makes the climb to the top.

The swap

Many service offerings are actually tightly-integrated bundles of services that are complementary to each other. When one is needed, the other almost always is. One of them tends to be the core service generating the primary demand. The others tend to be secondary and supporting. A set of multiple outcomes and experiences is packaged together and offered at a single price, and therefore there is a single consolidated net value associated with the entire package. However, the services within the package are by nature very different from one another, and therefore their designs are different. The capabilities, resources, artifacts, and events are different. The arrangements and agreements are different, as are the engagement and fulfillment sequences. Customers respond differently toward changes, especially when they don't seem to like improvements.

Furthermore, different departments, operational units, or even subcontractors and partners, may be responsible for the different components of the service package. Technological advances, new rules and regulations, and new norms, may apply to one component but not to others. All this creates tensions, and service providers find it difficult to manage the different motivations and expectations of customers for the services within the package. Service providers may find it best to unbundle the package and offer the services as separately priced options, some of which may already have been outsourced to third parties. Now each spun-off service has its own net value pair, which may fall in different regions. Customers and service providers can now negotiate them separately. Let's say the package is split into two services, one the core, and the other supporting. Customers may be more sensitive to changes in outcomes, experiences, and pricing in the case of one, compared to the other. It's possible to end up in a situation where service providers enjoy a much higher net value in one, and a much lower net value in the other. What service providers can then do is to offset the imbalances. They can perform a swap. They can make changes and improvements that progressively move from one end to the other, simultaneously moving the other services in the opposite direction.

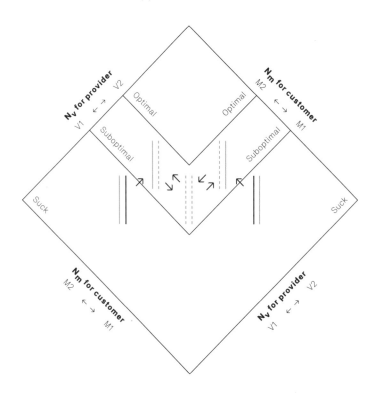

Figure 49
The swap

——— Great
------- Ok
——— Not ok

What happens in the absence of strategic design? Net values for both sides can be dismal – below both sets of thresholds. How did they get there in the first place? As with success, there are many paths to failure. We can imagine that net values gradually worsened over time in a downward spiral. Customers often respond with spending cuts. Feedback loops often have a delay, which makes corrective actions too little too late, or they overcompensate. As customers and service providers assess their

Downward spiral

net values, revise their expectations, and adjust their outlook, they may inadvertently trigger the downward spiral, and net values begin to oscillate. It may all start with one bad compromise in the design of the service. Instead of moving northeast or northwest, the net values go south. Depending on the nature of the service, and the quality of the design, things can go quickly from good to ugly, with the flaring up of unintended conflict. This could happen within a large outsourcing contract, between two organizations. But that would be due to an abject lack of transparency and trust. It is more likely to happen to consumer services, where customers are numerous, and are more likely to simply leave, than sit across a conference table and negotiate. It's worse when the services produce commodity outcomes that customers can readily procure from other providers.

Figure 50
Downward spiral,
tactical movement

Great ——
Ok ------
Not ok ——

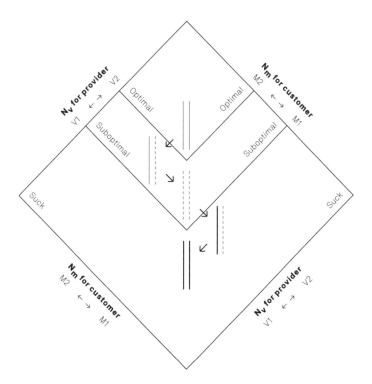

Quite often, downward spirals are set off by aggressive measures aimed at reducing waste, eliminating unnecessary steps, and making operations lean. There is always the risk of going too far but not realizing it because the adverse effect is on the other side. Services are very different from manufacturing, mining, and agriculture. Outcomes and experiences are products of supply and demand that materialize in situ and just in time, along a locus. There is a relatively higher level of residual uncertainty in every instance of performance and affordance. Therefore, efforts to improve efficiency on one side should carefully consider the impact on the overall design, and the net values on both sides.

30 years ago, Herbert Simon wrote: »Everyone designs who devises courses of action aimed at changing existing situations into preferred ones.« The upward spiral, the hook, and the swap are examples of courses of action aimed at changing an existing set of N values to a preferred set.

Service design

Strategy is a devised course of action – the most prudent path – toward higher net values for both sides. Therefore, strategy is design.

The 16x frame and the O-P/E=N equation are useful in translating strategy to service design. Moving the N values across the three levels or nine regions requires improvements to the qualities of outcome, price, and experience – the O, P, and E numbers. Those changes are made by devising courses of action that we have been calling performances and affordances which are further broken down into courses of action that map to the 16 elements of design.

Thus, the smallest of changes – whether to dialog and interaction, touchpoints and interfaces, facilities and infrastructure, to policies and procedures, or to terms and conditions, to give a few examples – are small vectors of improvement that add up to new net values that translate into movement on a map.

Design is the ultimate
expression of strategy.

The design of performances and affordances for outcomes that satisfy customer needs; and experiences
that give the highest possible net values at the lowest
possible price.

10

Closing

10

The Sunshine Cab Company is a service company owned by the vehicles. Each autonomous vehicle is a legal person recognized by law – i.e., they can acquire property, conclude contracts, and be sued for damage. Machines own and operate Sunshine, filling the roles of service provider and agent (MM). Their customers and users are humans (HH). They have the reputation of being the quickest, safest, and most dependable taxi service. They're especially known for their patience, politeness, and safe driving. With their HHMM model, they effectively compete with services that have humans on both sides (HHHH).

Sunshine has signed a series of contracts with service providers that support its operations. One company finds riders, provides dispatch, optimizes routing, adjusts pricing, and handles payments. Another provides maintenance, repair, and overhaul and garages for parking. And yet another provides machine learning experience – so the driving gets better over time, attracting customers, reducing operational risks, and earning discounts on insurance premiums.

Sunshine also retains the services of a white-shoe law firm to represent them in all matters and protect their interests, including negotiating contracts and defending them in court. An accounting firm helps with all financial matters, including taxes. A security firm monitors and protects them from all kinds of threats, including vandalism and hacking. As taxpayers they also benefit from regular law enforcement.

Double Helix is a design studio and consultancy that offers »Designcoding«. They specialize in HHMM contracts. For their clients they develop hundreds of 16x frames that cover the

**The Sunshine Cab
Company**

entire service operation. The frames are the 'source code' for everything, from the proprietary software that powers the enterprise, to the policies, procedures, and protocols for engaging with humans and other machines. A measurement system based on the O-P/E=N equation is used to evaluate changes to design. The agency receives a bonus based on the number of weeks during which net values are in optimal regions.

This of course is fiction, but who knows how far we are from it. As designer, filmmaker, and futurist Anab Jain proclaims, »other worlds are possible«.

Meanwhile, the universe of services continues to expand in all sort of directions, creating new service worlds. We have to prepare for the new problem spaces those expansions uncover. We already have services that are everywhere, know everything, and have the power to shape our societies. Omnipresent, omniscient, and omnipotent are words scriptures use to describe gods, goddesses, and supreme beings. After a few episodes of the Netflix series Black Mirror, one might wonder if those words also describe some services.

> » We shape our buildings, thereafter they shape us.«

> —
>
> Winston Churchill

We shape our services, thereafter they shape us. They influence our perceptions of the world around us, how we interact with each other, and how we govern ourselves through democracies. They shape our markets, our work places, and our living environments. We need new tools, skills, and practices to shape our services. We have to design them to be strong and flexible structures that won't easily fail.

Bridges are strong and flexible structures withstanding varying loads as traffic flows across them. By analyzing stress and strain under dynamic loading, we optimize their designs. Like bridges, services may have different »shapes and sizes« but they all essentially close gaps. Socioeconomic structures connecting two sides. Symmetry and balance are necessary to distribute the dynamic loads of demand and supply, across a span. Strategic industry factors – costs and risks peculiar to a sector,

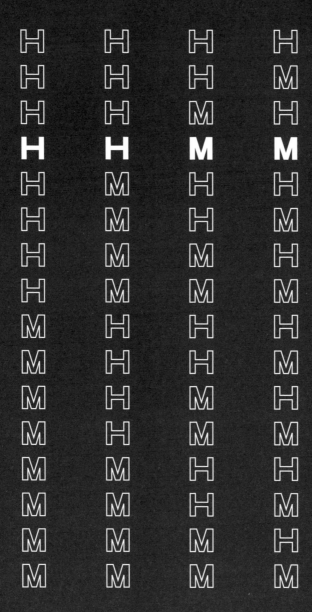

SERVICE CONTRACTS

including competition, public policy, regulation, technologies, and trends – define the traffic, terrain, and climate.

It takes years for new ways of thinking to become norm. Take graphical user interfaces and object-oriented programming, for example. Therefore, to advance the thinking in services, we must start now. The patterns, principles, and templates in this book are for you to apply in your practices now. Make them your own, put them to new uses, and improvise. Or, throw them away, when you are no longer satisfied. Chances are you will develop something better. In fact, one of the many reasons for publishing these methods in this book is to encourage others to further develop them.

For example, the stereotypes and the spectrum presented in chapter 3 are potentially the basis for a full-fledged pattern language, or perhaps for messaging protocols used in cloud computing and IoT. The 'executable script' shown in chapter 7 may inspire someone to develop the next-generation customer journey map that is addressable, programmable, and machine-readable. The 16x frame can act as filter embedded with design logic, between the fuzzy front end full of incomplete, unclear, and ambiguous customer needs and the backlog for product development. O-P/E=N can be further developed to create new types of metrics, benchmarks, and risk analysis.

Who knows.

Acknowledgements

There are several who made this book possible. As publisher, Bionda Dias gave me valuable advice, while also reminding me to relax, enjoy the writing, and have fun. When I met Anna Ranches and Helene Uhl, I knew they are the ones to give this book its final form, with their talent, experience, and love of print design. I'm glad Johanna Schwarzer joined their team just in time.

David Nyman played the role of editor and producer, always keeping you, the reader, in mind. He spent countless hours catching errors, and patiently helping me understand structural problems. Dounia Ouchene helped me scope the book, pick a title, and define its purpose. The book is better because of them. Also because of Dave Hora, Stephan Jenniskens, Gene Moy, James Jones, Zach Hyman, Svante Brehmer, Michael Mirbaha, Björn Hägglund, Ben Kraal, Johan Alviander, Nicolae Naumof, Jack Bischof, Jan van Winsen, Ben ten Dam, Lodewijk Bonebakker, Elisa Giaccardi, Sarah Fathallah, Antonio Starnino, Mark Burgess, and Danny Buerkli. They were kind enough to be reviewers. Mark Langedijk, Ruud Staijen, Marcel van Breeden, and Adrian Brown gave research input on certain topics.

Those who took part in the many workshops and projects I ran, will perhaps only now realize their indirect contributions. Their names are too many to list, but their participation was made possible by: Maarten Hillenaar, Leon-Paul de Rouw, Hans Hendriks, Richard Hilhorst, Wijnand Lodder, Peter Blom, Robert Bennis, Els van Engelen, Wouter Breedveld, Rianne Blacquière, Mariet Mevis, Ko Mies, and Brian Johnson; Hank Marquis; Deepa Gill, Joye Jepson, Sandra Jeffcoat, Lisa Valle, and Ted Colbert III; Marian Poolen, Harmen Harmsma, and Ric de Rooij; Harmen Alkema, Hugo Butter, Gerrit Jan van 't Eind, Jaap Velzel, Mo Jaber, and Ruud Staijen; Svante Brehmer, Michael Mirbaha, Johan Alviander, and Thomas Lagerfeldt; Pieter Nieuweboer, Tom van Sante, Michiel Struijk, Jeannette Kalfsterman, and Geert Rensen; Brandon Rowberry and Chris Finlay.

Thank you Fathima, Ammi, Abba, Ali, Amaan, Esa, Sajid, Naveed, and Amjad for your love and support.

11

Appendix

11

Bibliography

A
Alexander, C., Ishikawa, S., & Silverstein, M. (1977). A Pattern Language: Towns, Buildings, Construction. Oxford University Press.

B
Brandes, N., & Brandes, D. (2011, December). In Retailing, Assortment is Job One. Harvard Business Review.
Brown, T. (2012, Spring). From Blueprint to Genetic Code: The Merits of an Evolutionary Approach to Design. The Rotman Magazine.
Burgess, M. (2015). Thinking in Promises: Designing systems for cooperation. O'Reilly Media.

C
Casais, M., Mugge, R., & Desmet, P. (2016). Meaningful Things: Exploring the Symbolic Meaning of the Material Environment and its Impact on Happiness.
Casais, M., Mugge, R. & Desmet, P.M.A. (2016). Berlin: North American Association for Consumer Research Conference (ACR) Film.
Cila, N., Giaccardi, E., Tynan-O'Mahony, F., & Speed, C. (2015). Thing-centered narratives: A study of object personas. Proceedings of the 3rd Seminar International Research Network for Design Anthropology. Aarhus.
Coppola, G. (2018, April 4). BMW Subscription Pilot Puts You in a Top Tier Car for $3,700 a Month. Retrieved from Bloomberg.com: https://www.bloomberg.com/news/articles/2018-04-04/bmw-pilot-puts-subscribers-in-performance-cars-at-3-700-a-month
CPI. (2016). The Public Impact Fundamentals Report. Centre for Public Impact.

D
Davis, J. L., & Chouinard, J. B. (2016, 12 1). Theorizing Affordances:

From Request to Refuse. Bulletin of Science, Technology & Society, pp. 241-248.

Dorst, K. (2015). Frame Innovation: Create new thinking by design. MIT Press.

Dorst, K., & Cross, N. (2001). Creativity in the design process: co-evolution of problem–solution. Design Studies, 22(5), 425–437.

E

Edvardsson, B., Gustafsson, A., Kristensson, P., Tronvoll, B., & Witell, L. (2014). New Service Development from the Perspective of Value Co-Creation. In R. T. Rust, & M.-H. Huang, Handbook of Service Marketing Research (pp. 346–369). Cheltenham: Edward Elgar.

G

Giaccardi, E., Cila, N., Speed, C., & Caldwell, M. (2016b). Thing Ethnography: Doing Design Research with Non-Humans. DIS ,16: Proceedings of the 2016 ACM Conference on Designing Interactive Systems (pp. 377-387). ACM Press.

Gibson, J. J. (1979). The Theory of Affordances: The Ecological Approach to Visual Perception. Hillsdale: Lawrence Erlbaum Associates.

Goodwin, T. (2015, March 4). The Battle Is For The Customer Interface. Retrieved from TechCrunch: https://techcrunch.com/2015/03/03/in-the-age-of-disintermediation-the-battle-is-all-for-the-customer-interface

H

Hara, K. (2007). Designing Design. Lars Müller Publishers.

Harari, Y. N. (2015). Sapiens: a Brief History of Humankind. HarperCollins Publishers.

I

Iqbal, M., & Nieves, M. (2007). ITIL: Service Strategy. London: TSO.

K

Kahneman, D., & Tversky, A. (1979). Prospect Theory: An Analysis of Decision under Risk. Econometrica, 47(2).

Kay, J. (2011). Obliquity: Why Our Goals Are Best Achieved Indirectly. Penguin Press.

Khazan, O. (2015, June 8). The Hospitals That Overcharge Patients by 1,000 Percent. The Atlantic.

M

Meadows, D. (2008). Thinking in Systems: A Primer. Chelsea Green Publishing.

Nørretranders, T. (1999). The User Illusion: cutting consciousness down to size. New York: Penguin Books.

N

Norman, D. A. (1988). The Psychology of Everyday Things. Basic Books.

O

Olson, T. (2017, March 12). Iteration is not design: Debunking design Darwinism. The Design Innovator.

R

Reeves, S., Kuper, A., & Hodges, B. D. (2008). Qualitative research methodologies: ethnography. BMJ, 337.

Rock, D., Grant, H., & Grey, J. (2016, September 22). Diverse Teams Feel Less Comfortable – and That's Why They Perform Better. Harvard Business Review.

Rozenblit, L., & Keil, F. C. (2002). The misunderstood limits of folk science: an illusion of explanatory depth. Cognitive Science, 26(5), 521-562.

S

Simon, H. A. (1962, Dec. 12). The Architecture of Complexity. Proceedings of the American Philosophical Society, 106(6), pp. 467-482.

Simon, H. A. (1996). The Sciences of the Artificial. MIT Press.

Szabo, N. (1996). Smart Contracts: Building Blocks for Digital Markets. Retrieved from http://www.fon.hum.uva.nl/rob/Courses/InformationInSpeech/CDROM/Literature/LOTwinterschool2006/szabo.best.vwh.net/smart_contracts_2.html

T

Thompson, D. (2018, February 17). Airbnb and the Unintended Consequences of ‚Disruption'. The Atlantic.

X

Xu, T., Park, A., Bai, G., & et al. (2017). Variation in Emergency Department vs Internal Medicine Excess Charges in the United States. JAMA Internal Medicine, 1139–1145.

End notes

1   Depending on our political views, we have different ways of ratio-
nalizing government spending on portfolios such as defense, foreign affairs, and intelligence. As taxpayers, how do we know what
we are getting? What is the fair price to pay for an air force to de-
fend the skies? How much should we spend to protect a sensitive
ecosystem, or to keep the air and water clean? Little or nothing,
some might argue. At all costs, others might say.

2   It is often difficult to find someone capable and trustworthy and
arrange for them to do the work by instructions and permissions.
All that has been made relatively risk-free and convenient by an
entire category of services based on anthropologistics: the logistics of finding, fetching, routing, and putting someone in a position to accomplish a task on time. The task and the terms and
conditions are based on templates. Third-party services process
payments. Support teams handle errors and exceptions, and
settle disputes. The service providers charge a small fee that's
either a fixed amount or a fixed percentage of the value of the
transaction.

3   In theory, an airline can operate without owning anything except
customer relationships and a brand. It can lease or rent the most
expensive assets: aircraft and engines. Airports offer infrastructures and facilities as-a-service including a security perimeter,
hangars, runways, and gates. They offer time slots and landing
rights. Baggage handling, ticketing, and reservation systems are
available as services. As is fueling, catering, and other ground operations. Airport staff, pilots and cabin crew can be contractors,
not employees. Code sharing with other airlines. Air traffic control is a service. All the airline has to do is sell tickets.

4   GDPR is already making privacy a much more tangible thing. Websites make digital content available free-of-charge because visi-
tors give consent to the storing of bits of information that allows
services to track users, observe and analyses their habits and
preferences, and collect data for commercial use by third-parties. GDPR rules went into effect on May 25, 2018. They aim to protect the privacy of EU citizens worldwide. They also give people
greater control over the use of their personal data. The misuse of
their data will attract penalties and fines.

5   The agency problem is due to the conflicts that arise when one
party (the agent), acting on behalf of another party (the princi-

pal), recommends or pursues courses of action that further their own interests. Mechanics, doctors, and lawyers, for example, may push for repairs, treatments, or legal options that are costly and unnecessary, but fetch them higher fees. We now see the emergence of a new kind of agents – personal assistants such as Alexa, Siri, and Google – who perform tasks that involve using other services to look up things and make purchases, on behalf of the household. But they are also agents of Amazon, Apple, and Google, collecting data on the household's needs, habits, and preferences. Data that is then offered to third-parties for commercial use.

Hospitals and physicians have enormous power over the people they treat. They are entrusted to act with honesty and integrity. However, bad actors burden the systems they operate in, with unnecessary costs that have no impact on the quality of patient outcomes. One study found that, in 2012, the 50 U.S. hospitals with the highest mark-ups, charged 10 times more than the cost of treatment (Khazan, 2015). According to a study published in *The Journal of the American Medical Association, Internal Medicine*, adult patients receiving emergency care were charged 340 percent more than what the government-run Medicare pays, for procedures such as suturing a wound and interpreting a head CT scan (Xu, Park, Bai, & et al, 2017).   **6**

Services act upon or perform work on something that is of value to the customer. The performance makes that thing more useful and therefore more valuable. In the case of transportation, the physical coordinates of the passenger are the »thing« the service acts upon, gradually modifying them to match those of the destination.   **7**

What Jerry was going to mention before Tom interrupted him was the book *The Theory of Affordances: The Ecological Approach to Visual Perception* in which James Gibson, its author, introduces the word *affordance* to explain that which an *environment* offers to the *animal* (Gibson, 1979). It was a new word Gibson felt compelled to make up at that time. As an ecological psychologist, he spoke in terms of affordances being relative to the animal and the environment. That is, different animals perceive a different set of affordances in the same terrain. Affordance has a different meaning in interaction design given by usability expert Donald Norman (Norman, 1988): »*An affordance is the design as-*   **8** pect of an object which suggest how the object should be used; a visual clue to its function and use.« In this book, the concept of affordance is Gibsonian: Things are available to other things. For example, tracks allow trains passage and give traction. The designs of the train and the tracks create the affordance by allowing the two things to interact. By expanding our concept of »things« to include intangible ones such as identity, privacy, and security, we can apply the concept of affordance to all kinds of services.

9   General Motors, Porsche, and BMW, for example, allow customers to subscribe to a fleet of luxury vehicles. The subscriptions offer far greater affordances than traditional leases. The monthly fee reflects that. It is nearly three times a lease payment. However, that is not a fair comparison. Customers are subscribing to an entire fleet, not just one vehicle. They can choose whichever type of vehicle they fancy, then swap it for something more suitable for a different occasion. Apps, maps, and white gloves make the exchange quick and convenient. The fee also covers insurance, maintenance and roadside assistance (Coppola, 2018).

10   The schedule shapes the overall affordance of the tram system. On any given day, riders across the system may choose to appear at any stop, within a time slot, and demand to be taken from there to any other stop. Seats or standing room are to be made available for every possible journey between the two stops, whichever two they might be. Everything the tram company does in terms of planning and optimization, is towards increasing the overall affordance.

11   Here Tom invokes the idea of *exformation*, that is »the discarded information, everything we do not actually say but have in our heads when or before we say anything at all.« (Nørretranders, 1999)

12   At a 2017 conference in Paris, at the Organization for Economic Cooperation Development, this author was duly impressed by how live translation services go to work. The facilities are staffed with a team of translators in a glass balcony at the back of the room, with speakers directly ahead of them. It is a permanent arrangement that includes high-quality audio equipment that wirelessly streams the translations live through multiple channels. Every chair in the audience has a pouch with a receiver and headphones.

According to Investopedia, »An asset is a resource with economic value that an individual, corporation or country owns or controls with the expectation that it will provide a future benefit.« Here we extend the definition of asset to include things that hold symbolic meaning in the form of memories of good times or reminders of personal beliefs, aspirations, and successes. Things that contribute to the subjective well-being of individuals (Casais, Mugge, & Desmet, 2016). Things that are priceless. Or things that are simply collectibles such as Beanie Babies and Blockchain-based Crypto Kitties.

13

Shortcomings and shortfalls have similarities and differences. Both indicate things are »*short*« of their full potential. Both suggest a thing could be more useful and valuable in another condition or state. The difference is, a thing with a shortcoming needs »*to be*« rendered to a preferred condition or state. A thing with a shortfall needs »*to have*« access to a resource. Shortcomings can cause shortfalls. For example, hospital linen such as scrubs and gowns have shortcomings when they are soiled from use. They need »*to be*« cleaned and sterilized. Hospital staff then need »*to have*« clean linen to change into. As they grab a fresh set, they create shortfalls in the clean closet which then needs »to have« replenishments. Shortfalls can cause shortcomings. Purchases need »*to have*« payment authorizations at points of sale. Amounts from account balances then need »*to be*« authorized by the banks.

14

The availability of a resource by itself is meaningless if there isn't any access to it, or if access is so costly or difficult that it is simply not worth it from the customer's point of view. Similarly, having access by itself is worthless if the resource isn't dependably available when needed, or in the desired quality or quantity. Goods at a retail store are a bit more expensive than at a factory outlet, due to the convenient access. Availability is all-important in the retail business. If two retail stores are side by side, the one with the better assortment of goods usually wins (Brandes & Brandes, 2011). Also, digital things can be more easily made available at more places and in more ways and often at a lower cost than their more »physical« equivalents. Fintech startups have been successful partly because the convenience of access their services afford through mobile apps.

15

16   If we look at a busy airport with child-like imagination, we may see aircraft as human – personifying them as in the Disney movie *Planes* (2013). Some look serious, others have smiley faces. Busy, industrious, and important, everything revolves around them on the airside of operations. Jet ways, ramps, trucks, tractors and highloaders attend to them from nose to tail. Their paths are kept clear. They give everything they've got during take-off, tough it through turbulence, and absorb impact during landing. We monitor them for stress and strain, and bring them in for preventive care. (Airplane health management is actually a service.) We paint them in beautiful colors. Pilots use terms of endearment when referring to them. We celebrate their years of service. We retire them.

17   Autographers are small cameras that are clipped to a person or object and automatically take pictures when prompted by one of the sensors embedded in them (accelerometer, color sensor, magnetometer, thermometer, and PIR). The Autographer data provide time-lapse details that can be accumulated into a visual narrative of events and objects. (Cila, Giaccardi, Tynan-O'Mahony, & Speed, 2015)

18   The Royal Netherlands Marechaussee safeguards the security of the State, both in the Netherlands and further afield. It is deployed at locations of strategic importance. From royal palaces to the external borders of Europe. From airports in the Netherlands to theatres of war and crisis areas all over the world. The force is flexible, robust and deployable in any situation. It is a gendarmerie corps: a police force with military status. [Source: https://www.defensie.nl/organisatie/marechaussee]

19   Schiphol Airport has been one of the 12 partners in the recently concluded PASSME Project funded by the European Union's Horizon 2020 research and innovation program (grant agreement No. 636308), along with KLM and the Delft University of Technology (TU/Delft). The goal was to find ways to reduce by 60 minutes the overall travel time for passengers across European airports. Four breakthroughs have been developed: (1) A forecast system that predicts 30 minutes ahead of time passenger demand at different points of the airport, so airport managers can add staff or open additional lanes. (2) A new service concept that allows passengers and their bags to travel separately from door-to-door, entirely bypassing the regular pathways through the airport. (3)

Laterally adjustable aircraft seats to speed up the boarding process, carts that go through security checks, and waiting areas
all reduce the stress and improve comfort. (4) A smartphone app
that helps passengers get all the information they need during
their entire journey. At app also monitors their stress levels and
tells them to relax when they anxious due to the lack of information about gates, boarding times, and baggage carousels.
[https://passme.eu]

The bags have done their job so far of holding her personal be-   **20**
longings, making them convenient to walk with, and protecting
them from damage. They have been strong and sturdy assets.
However, when she arrives at the airport check-in counter, the
bags suddenly find themselves suffering shortcomings and
shortfalls. Shortcomings because they need to be ticketed,
screened, and transported. Shortfalls because they need to
have bag tags, security clearance, and secure passage to the aircraft's hold. In that context, the bags are unable to further realize
their potential as strong and sturdy assets.

The International Air Transport Association (IATA) is the trade as-   **21**
sociation for the world's airlines, representing some 290 airlines
or 82% of total air traffic. They help formulate industry policy on
critical aviation issues, so airlines can operate safely, securely,
efficiently, and economically under clearly defined rules. Simplifying processes and increasing passenger convenience while
reducing costs and improving efficiency is a key mission. Standards are critical to interoperability which in turn is critical to the
viability of service ecosystems.

Cloud-based or cloud computing simply mean, your apps and   **22**
data »come alive, thrive, and survive« on a service provider's infrastructure, instead of one that you own, operate, and manage.
You have fast and secure access to your apps and data via the
Internet. All the time, and from anywhere. You can give access
privileges to whoever you want, including your employees, customers, citizens, family or friends. Millions of computers may
together form a single »cloud.« The capacity is available on-
demand in metered units. Customers only pay for the capacity
they use. There is no minimum commitment. If you need more capacity – suddenly or gradually – it is immediately from the nearest facility within an availability zone. For example, AWS has 54
availability zones across 18 geographic regions.

23   Compare the way Netflix delivers video on demand today to the time it was mailing digital video discs via the US Postal Service. Only one customer at a time could enjoy a DVD. Several copies were necessary to support the popularity of a title. Discs would suffer damage and replacements would take time. One way to cover carrying costs was to charge a premium for the option of having more than one DVD out at a time. However, not everybody was willing to pay for that privilege. Binge-watching parties could not be thing. Imagine what a postal strike meant. Therefore, the only conceivable way for Netflix to grow into what it is today, was to go from renting video to projecting it on private screens. »Your own private projectionist.«

24   Viewers around the world watch Netflix on many different kinds of devices. Therefore, for each item on its catalog Netflix must first create over 50 different versions from a master file, one for each type of device, screen size, and bit rate (depending on the speed of the Internet connection). This transcoding process requires a significant amount of computing power Netflix dynamically gets »in the cloud«.

25   In services that deliver digital content, such as live or on-demand video and music, reducing buffer time (the time between hitting the play button and the video playing) is all-important. Latency and network congestion are causes of service failure. Therefore, storing local copies of the content, close to where users are mostly likely to demand access from, is part of the strategic design of such services. It is why content delivery networks, such as CloudFront, Akamai, and Limelight Networks play such an important role. Netflix saw this problem early on and started distributing copies on special hardware it designed for the purpose and place them in the data centers of local Internet service providers (ISP).

26   ING-THING is also the name of the word game developed for workshops on »thinking in services«. Participants get two types of cards: the ING cards with verbs (in present participle) and THING cards with nouns on them. Players form verb-noun pairs that describe the essence of a service. For example, transporting-goods, verifying-information, and repairing-equipment. Those with ING cards are service providers with revenue targets. Those with THING cards are customers with budgets. At the start of each round, a facilitator reads aloud a story in which a service solves a problem and saves the day. Players make note of verbs and nouns in the story to prepare their ING and THING cards for that round. Customers allocate their budgets across the THING cards they are going to play. Service providers do the same with their ING cards and revenue targets. In doing so they price their service offerings. Players take turns to put down an ING or a THING. The next player in turn tries to match the card – ING for a THING; THING for an ING. If the word pair describes performance or affordance that fits the story, both players get 5 points each. If the budget on the THING card is greater than or equal to the price on the ING card, they each get 20 additional points. The arguments that ensue are insightful, and fun.

The company Iron Mountain fulfills a need many organizations have: to archive documents while freeing up office space on expensive real estate. Iron Mountain collects documents from customer premises and stores them at offsite locations. It also helps customers comply with rules and regulations with regards to retention. That includes the shredding of documents to maintain privacy and confidentiality. Herman Knaust, its founder, started by convincing the East River Savings Bank to let his company take care of the safekeeping of microfilm copies of deposit records and duplicate signature cards. He put them in storage vaults inside an abandoned iron ore mine, under a mountain. Soon the company grew to be a market leader in the protection of vital records. They now cover the entire lifecycle of vital records. They even help customers eliminate unnecessary documents and records. They have four data centers for storing and serving documents and records. They have facilities compliant with regulations on handling protected health information. Hollywood studios such as Universal Studios and Paramount Pictures depend on them for archiving valuable assets.

27

The Svalbard Global Seed Vault: »Deep inside a mountain on a remote island in the Svalbard archipelago, halfway between mainland Norway and the North Pole, lies the Global Seed Vault. It is a long-term seed storage facility, built to stand the test of time – and the challenge of natural or man-made disasters. The Seed Vault represents the world's largest collection of crop diversity. Worldwide, more than 1700 genebanks hold collections of food crops for safekeeping, yet many of these are vulnerable, exposed not only to natural catastrophes and war, but also to avoidable disasters, such as lack of funding or poor management. Some-

28

Figure 51
Affordance of permafrost

thing as mundane as a poorly functioning freezer can ruin an entire collection. And the loss of a crop variety is as irreversible as the extinction of a dinosaur, animal or any form of life. It was the recognition of the vulnerability of the world's genebanks that sparked the idea of establishing a global seed vault to serve as a backup storage facility. The purpose of the Vault is to store duplicates (backups) of seed samples from the world's crop collections.« [Source: https://www.croptrust.org]. In 2017 the unthinkable happened. Extraordinarily hot Arctic temperatures due to climate change caused melting and water breached the vault entrance. The affordance of permafrost is now at risk. The irony is inescapable.

29 For example, upon request, the Amazon AWS Lambda service »runs« a registered piece of software code or »function«. Every time an event in the outside world invokes the function, Lambda executes a set of instructions. To do that, it automatically provisions all the resources necessary to get the job done. This is serverless computing. Customers do not have to worry about forecasting their capacity requirements. They simply pay for the number of times the code runs and the resources it actually consumes during each event. Measurements are in gigabyte-seconds (GB-seconds) – rounded off to the nearest 100 milliseconds. For example, if a software function requiring 512MB of memory (0.5 GB) executes 3 million times in one month, and it runs for 1 second in each instance, the charges would be $18.34 for the performance (TT-4) and $0.40 for the affordance (HH-6), for a total of $18.74 per month. [Source: https://aws.amazon.com/lambda/pricing/]

30 In this pattern *events* are flowing or passing through a resource. By allowing them safe and sure passage, the resource is effectively conducting and conveying them. The events move under their own motive power. In other words, it isn't the job of the resource to expend energy to move them or change their coordinates (as in TT-4).

31 About 99% of data traffic between the United States and Europe flows through fiber-optic cables at the bottom of oceans. The Google-backed FASTER cable, for example, has a bandwidth of up to 60 Terabits/second. Then there is the Amazon AWS Snowball service. It can transfer petabytes of data by loading it onto high-capacity storage appliances, stacking those in shipping containers on trucks, and transporting them to a data center; entirely bypassing the Internet. As Ross Perot did in the 1960s, using magnetic tapes to transfer data between mainframes, when he founded EDS.

NATS is responsible for air traffic control in the UK airspace, of which just the Shanwick OCA is an expanse of 700,000 square miles of sky through which 1,400 flights fly daily across the North East Atlantic, during a summer day. That's made possible because NATS allocates airspace in the form of a corridor formed by creating separation between aircraft of a few nautical miles and several minutes apart, the exact numbers varying depending on the type of aircraft and sectors. The Shanwick OCA is the busiest of all areas in the North Atlantic Airspace, carrying around 80% of the region's traffic. [Source: www.nats.aero] **32**

The diplomatic channel is providing safe and secure passage for sensitive information. In general, conduits such as bridges, tunnels, and cables, provide insulation from outside noise or interference. What kind of environment, terrain, or surrounding space they allow passage through is as important as which two points they connect. The value increases with the carrying distance. **33**

In pattern 5 (CC) things are *traffic*. Here they are tenants. The primary value here is from having a conducive environment to stay in. Two spaces at the same location may have a price difference because one has more in terms of the accommodation, amenities, or the ambience. Two identical environments may have a price difference because one is at a location that is more popular or convenient. **34**

Take for example the difference between hiring a taxi (a chauffeured vehicle) and renting a car. Both solutions may serve the purpose, but, from a certain perspective, customers have far more flexibility and control with the rental car than they do with the taxi. The degree of affordance is even greater if the customer leases the vehicle. In that case, they »own« the vehicle for all practical purposes. The value of a vehicle depreciates with every mile driven. Since leases are based on fixed monthly payments, the service provider places a limit on the annual mileage. Leasing companies own some of the largest and youngest fleets of aircraft. It may be more prudent to lease or rent office space, than to own it. In many cases, ownership isn't even an option. Panav- **35** ision cameras, for example, are famously only available for rent. Borrowing money is like renting it. Borrowers return the principal amount, and the interest covers the »rental fee« and the cost of insuring against the risks of loan default.

36   This pattern broadly covers acquiring tangible and intangible goods from services. Whether from screens or displays; from cables, pipes, and sockets, including the growing number of charging points for electric vehicles; from streams of audio, video, and text; or from store shelves. Watching live events, listening to lectures or sermons, and receiving professional advice, are also examples of acquiring goods through services. We receive privileges and permissions in the form of tickets, tokens, and QR codes. Sometimes, simply from the opening of a door, removing of a barrier, or a nod from a sentry. From the mere presence of police officers, we receive assurances that induce feelings of safety, security, and peace of mind.

37   The canal is managed by Rijkswaterstaat – an agency of the Dutch Ministry of Infrastructure and Water Management, managing roads and waterways since 1798, including their design, construction, and maintenance. The agency was also responsible for developing the rail network. Today, as it looks towards the future, the agency faces new challenges in relation to mobility, safety and sustainability. Many of parts of the infrastructure, being intensively used, are reaching the end of their useful lives. The challenge for Rijkswaterstaat is to find a smart way of replacing these objects so that they can continue to serve the purpose of the networks in the future. [Source: https://www.rijkswaterstaat.nl/english/about-us/index.aspx]

38   Take for example these five services: A government officer inspecting a farm and issuing a rating; a private firm launching a satellite and placing it in orbit; a firm trading on the stock market on behalf of a pension fund; a team of surgeons performing hip replacement surgery to improve the quality of life of a patient; and a service streaming music on demand to liven up a living room. They are all quite different in terms of the people and things involved, and therefore the costs and risks. It is understandable the agreements covering those services also differ a lot.

39   The part about »not to do or give« something is most interesting. Both sides promise not to do anything that creates difficul-

ty for each other or requires additional time and effort. It is why the designing services places so much emphasis on exchanges between users and agents, with the aim of eliminating unnecessary dialog and interactions. It is also service agreements include »rules of engagement« users and agents must follow. Policies, procedures, and protocols aim to reduce uncertainty and risk. While serving one customer, service providers are being mindful of the interests of others.

Take for example Planet, the firm Alice uses to gain insight and intelligence based on satellite imagery and historical stacks of data. With over 175 satellites in orbit, Planet is able to line scan the entirety of the Earth's landmass every single day. That opens up possibilities for customers to mark just about any area of interest across over 300 million square kilometers. In fulfilling those requests, Planet downloads and processes over 5 terabytes of data a day. It already has a stack of 500 images for every given location on Earth's landmass. Customers can use the Planet API to directly access the pre-processed, analysis-ready imagery from within their workflows. The data feeds the analytical models they build and run. Or, they can use the time-lapse and compare features of the Planet Explorer tool. The more they integrate the data from Planet into their work, the more frequently they request new images, to discover change. More pictures are taken by more satellites.

40

Herbert Simon was one of the founding fathers of the behavioral school of economics, artificial intelligence, and organization science. He won the Sveriges Riksbank Prize in Economic Sciences in 1978 »for his pioneering research into the decision-making process within economic organizations.« His definition of »to design« is one of the most widely quoted. In his book, *The Sciences of the Artificial* (1969), Simon gave us a seven stage design process – define, research, ideate, prototype, choose, implement, and learn – that is still the basis of Design Thinking. Simon also co-founded the graduate school of industrial administration at Carnegie Mellon University. In his book, Economics: *The User's Guide* (2014), Ha-Joon Chang calls Simon »the last Renaissance man«.

41

Before, during, and after each period or cycle, the two sides evaluate their pains and gains. The pains could be more than expected, and the gains much less. Or, everything could turn out to be better than expected. It is important to note here that a given

42

set of outcomes, experiences, and price, depends on the design of the service. But the design isn't complete until the promises of demand are fitted in. This problem gives credibility to the idea that services are designed with customers, and never completely independent or ahead of them. The conundrum is that they are. It bears repeating: a service is never designed for a particular customer. Whatever is designed is then not a service. Therefore, it is only a question of how complete or incomplete the designs are, and that depends on the type of service.

43   In his book, *The Opposable Mind* (2007), Roger Martin defines Integrative Thinking as »the ability to face constructively the tension of opposing ideas and, instead of choosing one at the expense of the other, generate a creative resolution of the tension in the form of a new idea that contains elements of the opposing ideas but is superior to each.« American writer, F. Scott Fitzgerald went as far as to say: »The test of a first-rate intelligence is the ability to hold two opposed ideas in mind at the same time and still retain the ability to function.«

44   A key metric in the airline industry helps understand the duality of capability and resource. Available seat miles (ASM) are the number of aircraft seats available multiplied by the number of miles they are flown. For example, an aircraft with 100 seats flying a distance of 500 miles, produces 50000 ASM. Thus, the aircraft embodies resource and capability: Each seat is the resource. Each mile flown is the capability. An airline can add ASM to a route by adding more seats to a cabin configuration, or by operating additional flights. The same aircraft can produce more ASM on a longer route.

45   In theory, there are 40320 possible permutations from a set of eight narratives. That doesn't mean a team has to consider them all. It simply means there are so many ways to develop a good story, with a different start, middle, and end. It also means the same story can be retold in many different ways, with each version highlighting what's most important (for example, the chronology, progress in parallel, parts and counterparts, or the complications), from various perspectives such as: customer, user, provider or agent, performance, affordance, outcome, and experience. A particular order can make all the difference, and tell an entirely different story, because of the way it starts, how it progresses through the eight narratives, and how it ends.

The statement 1M: is common in the first two narratives, since both are from the same perspective: Khairun as a customer. In practice, several different observations form such statements. The final entry in the frame represents the reinforcement of similar observations, or reconciliation when the observations are different. In any case, the common statement binds the narratives together. Thus far the story covers the customer's perspective on the outcomes of performance and affordance.

46

A script as in the chain of cards that fed Joseph Marie Jacquard's textile loom with design patterns, or Herman Hollerith's punched cards that feeding data and programs to early computers. Think of a four-track tape that records and plays back the sound of the four promises – in the four notes of who, why, how and what. In that 2012 essay, Tim Brown goes on to suggest design should not be a static concept, but one that evolves and adapts over time (Brown, 2012). Using the examples of genetic code and software, he encourages designers to think in code. As we can see, that might be easier to do with the design of services.

47

Consensus is part of the culture in many organizations where making design more inclusive and integrative is considered to be of paramount importance. The earliest use cases of the 16x frame were within the Netherlands government, for achieving consensus between teams from different agencies and ministries, on the design of shared services such as those that provision digital work spaces for civil servants across the entire government. Achieving consensus in such a case is particularly important because the work environment can be very different for an inspector of roadways, bridges, and canals compared to that for a diplomat or a case worker administering welfare benefits.

48

What exactly are we buying when we buy a service? This point was raised in a 2010 memo by Dr. Ashton Carter, the former U.S. Secretary of Defense. At the time he was the Under Secretary in charge of Acquisition, Technology and Logistics. When buying weapon systems such as ships, tanks, and aircraft, you can at least »see the thing you're buying.« There are drawings, scale models, and prototypes. Experts can discuss very specific parameters of design and ask questions, such as the diameter of the gun or the tonnage of the ship. How far can the radar see? That is difficult to do with services. When it comes to services,

49

we don't exactly know what we're buying, Dr. Carter seems to suggest in that memo. It's difficult to be sure what comes in the box. Not just that, every time we open the box, the contents change slightly. On the other side of service contracts, providers face similar uncertainty and risk. What exactly are they putting into the box? In 2010, the U.S. Department of Defense (DoD) was facing budget cuts. It was spending over $200 billion on services across more than 100.000 contract vehicles. It was imperative for it to find ways to cut costs without compromising on the government's missions and objectives. The DoD couldn't afford the status quo, and if industry and government didn't find ways to together be more efficient, everybody stood to lose. Thus, the implementation of the DoD Better Buying Power (BBP) program, with the mission to improve the net value of those thousands of contracts. Under the overarching principle of »do more without more«, managers across the DoD seek cost-savings without compromise.

50   The back-end of the business of course is controlled by a few players with enormous scale in terms of data processing and network expanse, the likes of which are extremely hard to replicate. It remains to be seen to what extent blockchain technology and cryptocurrencies can mount a challenge. Government agencies that collect and distribute taxes are also in effect in the payments business. It is just that the services they process payments for are different in nature and paid for on a very different basis.

51   Scientists at the University of Minnesota have become the first in the world to perform magnetic resonance imaging (MRI) of the human body at 10.5 Tesla—a magnetic field strength 10 times greater than a standard MRI and topping even the most advanced scanners elsewhere in the world. The 110-ton magnet promises to produce scans at a finer level of detail, bringing new capabilities to scientists studying a wide range of diseases, such as Alzheimer's, heart disease, diabetes, and cancer.

52   Hospitals are wary of patients and hospital staff getting infections while getting or giving care and are therefore willing to go to great lengths to avoid such incidents. When there is an aversion to risk, the prospect of a loss outweighs that of an equivalent amount of gain. Therefore, hospitals are willing to pay for outcomes that reduce the prospect of such losses. How do we frame loss-avoidance as an enhancement or an enrichment? Being in a position of lower risk is effectively being better off. Therefore, the removal of risk is an enhancement. It's also why we pay for security, waste removal, and maintenance services. A reduction in the resources that are to be set aside to cover for the risk, is effectively an enrichment, in terms of the freed-up resources.

Whether airports independently provide a service to the passenger or act as the airline's agent to facilitate their service, depends on how you frame it. The same is true of all the other landside services such as baggage handling and security. Airlines do include all sorts of fees and taxes in the price of the ticket. At no point does a passenger directly pay the airport or any other service provider, except in the case of priority lanes, airport lounges, and in some cases, luggage trolleys. **53**

This problem is prevalent in consumer services – where customers and users are one and the same. The individual consumer has limited bargaining power, whereas enterprise customers can bring down the contractual hammer by stipulating penalties for delays. They are able to do that because service providers are given long-term contracts worth a lot more money than a consumer purchase. What is interesting is that, in the case of a scheduled flight, a loosely formed collective of passengers is actually the customer for a flight – a point earlier made with the explanation of why the fare is around $750 and not $75000. However, this collective does not have bargaining power because each ticket is a separate contract. **54**

Of course, it depends on the traveler and their purpose for travel. The same person while on vacation may not mind saving $350, which they may spend on food and accommodation. On some other occasion, this person may prefer arriving a bit more rested, or avoiding the chance of the connecting flight being delayed or cancelled, no matter how good a travel experience the airline may offer. Like Django. **55**

In his work on bounded rationality, a theory about economic decision-making, Herbert Simon uses the term »satisficing« – a combination of the words: »satisfy« and »suffice«. Simon argued that individuals do not seek to maximize their benefit from a particular course of action (since they cannot assimilate and digest all the **56** information that would be needed to do such a thing). Not only can they not get access to all the information required, but even if they could, their minds would be unable to process it properly. The human mind necessarily restricts itself. It is, as Simon put it, bounded by »cognitive limits«.

Index

BIS Publishers
Building Het Sieraad
Postjesweg 1
1057 DT Amsterdam
The Netherlands
T +31 (0)20 515 02 30
bis@bispublishers.com
www.bispublishers.com

ISBN is 978 90 6369 489 0

Copyright © 2018 Majid Iqbal

Produced by Insperio AB

Design by Bureau Mitte
www.bureaumitte.de